COMPLETE BOOK OF
Grade 3

THINKING
KIDS®

An Imprint of Carson-Dellosa LLC
P.O. Box 35665 • Greensboro, NC 27425 USA
carsondellosa.com

Thinking Kids®
Carson-Dellosa Publishing LLC
P.O. Box 35665
Greensboro, NC 27425 USA

ISBN 978-1-4838-1308-0

12 - 1261120

Dear Parents, Caregivers, and Educators,

The *Complete Book* series provides young learners an exciting and dynamic way to learn the basic skills essential to learning success. This vivid workbook will guide your student step-by-step through a variety of engaging and developmentally appropriate activities in phonics, reading comprehension, math, problem solving, and writing.

The *Complete Book of Grade 3* is designed for learning reinforcement and can be used as a tool for independent study. This workbook includes:

- High-interest lessons.
- Easy-to-understand examples and directions.
- Challenging concepts presented in simple language.
- Review lessons to measure progress and reinforce skills.
- Expanded teaching suggestions to guide further learning.

To find other learning materials that will interest your young learner and encourage school success, visit www.carsondellosa.com

4

Table of Contents

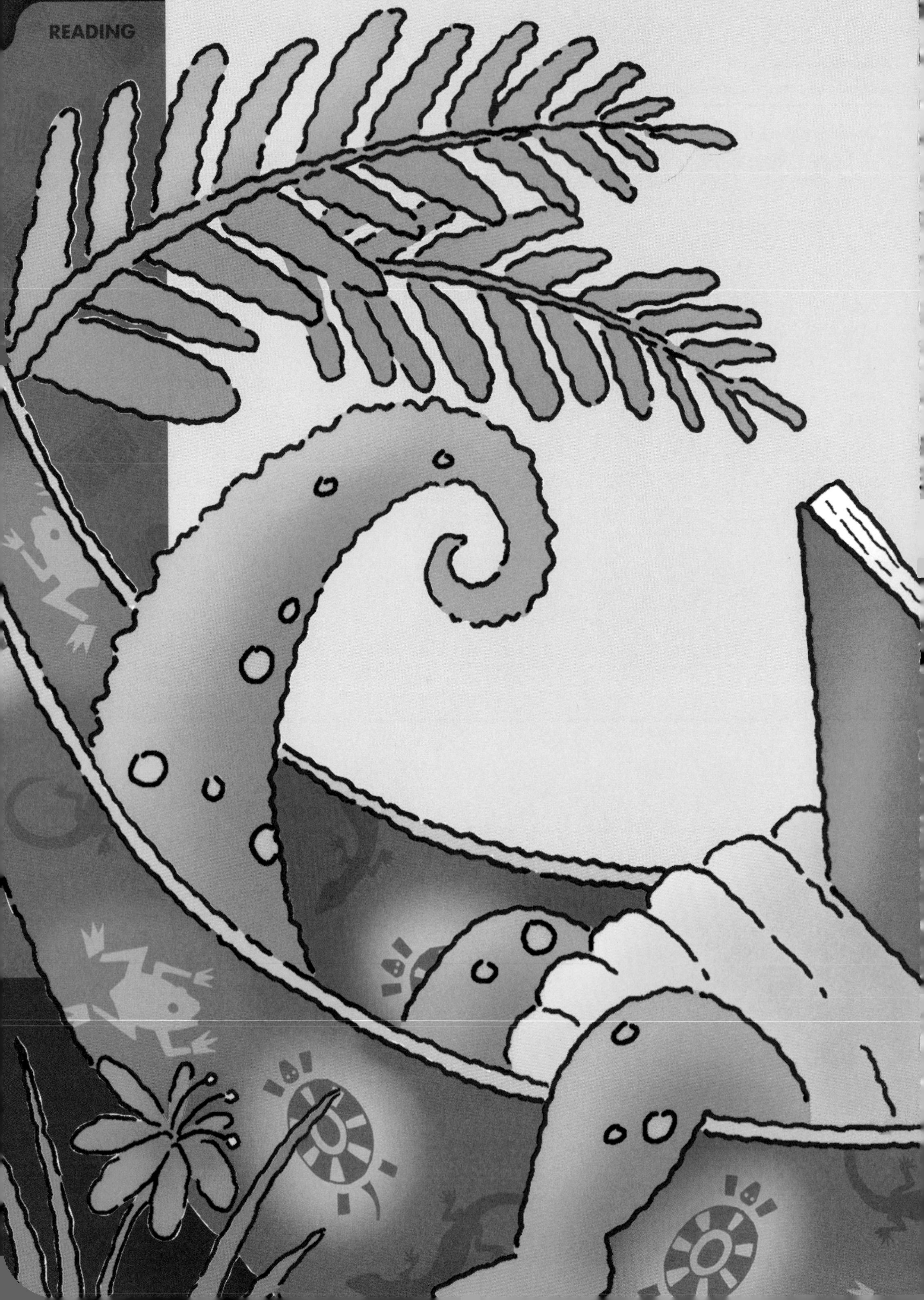

Reading

My Story

Directions: Fill in the blanks. Use these sentences to write a story about yourself.

I feel happy when _I sleep in bed_.

I feel sad when _I get no Popcorn_.

I am good at _Nothing_.

Words that describe me: _I love movie_

_____ _____

I can help at home by _Everything_

mry mom says.

My friends like me because _they are_

my friends.

I like to _play minecraft_

and fortnight

My favorite food is _pad thai_

My favorite animal is _Puppy_.

Now . . . take your answers and write a story about **you**!

Without a Sound

Some words are more difficult to read because they have one or more silent letters. Many words you already know are like this.

Examples: wrong and **night**.

Directions: Circle the silent letters in each word. The first one is done for you.

(w)rong	answer	autumn	whole
knife	hour	wrap	comb
sigh	straight	knee	known
lamb	taught	scent	daughter

Directions: Draw a line between the rhyming words. The first one is done for you.

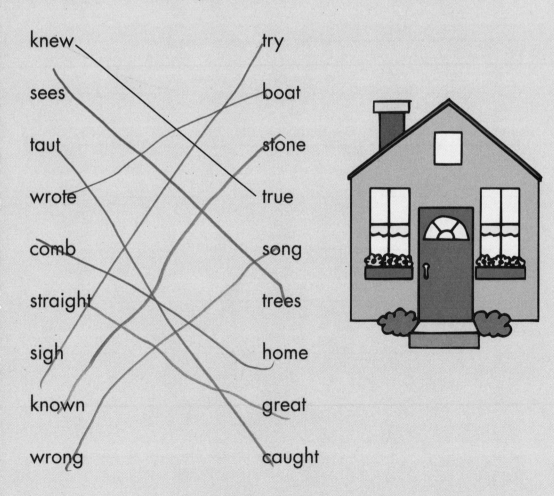

knew   try

sees   boat

taut   stone

wrote   true

comb   song

straight   trees

sigh   home

known   great

wrong   caught

The Long and Short of It

In some word "families," the vowels have a long sound when you would expect them to have a short sound. For example, the i has a short sound in **chill**, but a long sound in **child**. The **o** has a short sound in **cost**, but a long sound in **most**.

Directions: Read the words in the box below. Write the words that have a long vowel sound under the word **LONG**, and the words that have a short vowel sound under the word **SHORT**. (Remember, a long vowel says its name—like **a** in **ate**.)

old	odd	gosh	gold	sold
soft	toast	frost	lost	most
doll	roll	bone	done	kin
mill	mild	wild	blink	blind

LONG

bone
_____
_____
_____
_____
_____
_____
_____
_____

SHORT

doll
_____
_____
_____
_____
_____
_____
_____
_____

F Is for Fun!

Sometimes letters make sounds you don't expect. Two consonants can work together to make the sound of one consonant. The **f** sound can be made by **ph**, as in the word **elephant**. The consonants **gh** are most often silent, as in the words **night** and **though**. But they also can make the **f** sound as in the word **laugh**.

Directions: Circle the letters that make the f sound. Write the correct word from the box to complete each sentence.

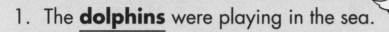

ele(ph)ant   cough   telephone   dolphins

enough   tough   alphabet   rough

1. The **dolphins** were playing in the sea.

2. Did you have _____ time to do your homework?

3. A cold can make you _____ and sneeze.

4. The _____ ate peanuts with his trunk.

5. The road to my school is _____ and bumpy.

6. You had a _____ call this morning.

7. The _____ meat was hard to chew.

8. The _____ has 26 letters in it.

Give Me a Break!

All words can be divided into syllables. Syllables are word parts which have one vowel sound in each part.

Directions: Draw a line between the syllable part and write the word on the correct line below. The first one is done for you.

lit|tle	bumblebee	pillow
truck	dazzle	dog
pencil	flag	angelic
rejoicing	ant	telephone

1 SYLLABLE

_____

_____

_____

_____

2 SYLLABLES

_____little_____

_____

_____

_____

3 SYLLABLES

_____

_____

_____

Razzle Dazzle

When the letters **le** come at the end of a word, they sometimes have the sound of **ul**, as in raffle.

Directions: Draw a line to match the syllables so they make words. The first one is done for you.

can	gle
tur	cle
pur	ple
cir	kle
spar	zle
raf	dle
ea	fle
siz	tle

Directions: Use the words you made to complete the sentences. One is done for you.

1. Will you buy a ticket for our school raffle?

2. The _____ pulled his head into his shell.

3. We could hear the bacon _____ in the pan.

4. The baby had one _____ on her birthday cake.

5. My favorite color is _____.

6. Look at that diamond _____!

7. The bald _____ is our national bird.

8. Draw a _____ around the correct answer.

It Takes Two

A compound word is two small words put together to make one new word. Compound words are usually divided into syllables between the two words.

Directions: Read the words. Then, divide them into syllables. The first one is done for you.

1. playground   _____ play   ground _____

2. sailboat   _____

3. doghouse   _____

4. dishpan   _____

5. pigpen   _____

6. outdoors   _____

7. beehive   _____

8. airplane   _____

9. hilltop   _____

10. broomstick   _____

11. sunburn   _____

12. oatmeal   _____

13. campfire   _____

14. somewhere   _____

Two in One

Directions: Read the compound words in the word box. Then use them to answer the questions. The first one is done for you.

sailboat	blueberry	bookcase	beehive
dishpan	pigpen	classroom	broomstick
treetop	fireplace	newspaper	sunburn

Which compound word means . . .

1. a case for books? _____bookcase_____

2. a berry that is blue? _____

3. a hive for bees? _____

4. a place for fires? _____

5. a pen for pigs? _____

6. a room for a class? _____

7. a pan for dishes? _____

8. a boat to sail? _____

9. a paper for news? _____

10. a burn from the sun? _____

11. the top of a tree? _____

12. a stick for a broom? _____

Play Ball!

Many words have more than one meaning. These words are called **multiple-meaning words**. Think of how the word is used in a sentence or story to determine the correct meaning.

Directions: The following baseball words have multiple meanings. Write the correct word in each baseball below.

play   bat   ball   fly   run

 This word means . . .

1. a flying mammal
2. a special stick used in baseball

 This word means . . .

1. a small insect
2. to soar through the air

 This word means . . .

1. a big dance
2. a round object used in sports

 This word means . . .

1. a performance
2. to amuse oneself

Which word is left? _____ Write sentences using two different meanings of the word.

1. _____

2. _____

Up to Bat

Directions: Complete each sentence using one of the words below.

bank   ball   park   run

play   kid   fly   bat

1. The kitten watched the _____
   crawl slowly up the wall.

2. "You wouldn't _____ me, would
   you?" asked Dad.

3. Do you think Aunt Donna and Uncle Mike will come to

   my school _____ ?

4. He hit the ball so hard it broke the

   _____ .

5. "My favorite part of the story is when the princess goes

   to the _____ ," sighed Veronica.

6. My brother scored the first _____
   in the game.

What's Next?

When words are in a certain order, they are in sequence.

Directions: Complete each sequence using a word from the box. There are extra words in the box. The first one has been done for you.

below	three
fifteen	December
twenty	above
after	go
third	hour
March	yard

1. January, February, _____March_____

2. before, during, _____

3. over, on, _____

4. come, stay, _____

5. second, minute, _____

6. first, second, _____

7. five, ten, _____

8. inch, foot, _____

Order, Order!

Directions: Fill in the blank spaces with what comes next in the series. The first one is done for you.

year	large	sixth	Wednesday
twenty	mile	night	paragraph
February	winter	seventeen	

1. Sunday, Monday, Tuesday, __Wednesday__

2. third, fourth, fifth, _____

3. November, December, January, _____

4. tiny, small, medium, _____

5. fourteen, fifteen, sixteen, _____

6. morning, afternoon, evening, _____

7. inch, foot, yard, _____

8. day, week, month, _____

9. spring, summer, autumn, _____

10. five, ten, fifteen, _____

11. letter, word, sentence, _____

What Happened?

Directions: Read each story. Circle the phrase that tells what happened before.

1. Anya is very happy now that she has someone to play with. She hopes that her new sister will grow up quickly!

   A few days ago . . .
   Anya was sick.
   Anya's mother had a baby.
   Anya got a new puppy.

2. Sara tried to mend the tear. She used a needle and thread to sew up the hole.

   While playing, Sara had . . .
   broken her bicycle.
   lost her watch.
   torn her shirt.

3. The movers took Diego's bike off the truck and put it in the garage. Next, they moved his bed into his new bedroom.

   Diego's family . . .
   bought a new house.
   went on vacation.
   bought a new truck.

4. Katie picked out a book about dinosaurs. Conner, who likes sports, chose two books about baseball.

   Katie and Conner . . .
   went to the library.
   went to the playground.
   went to the grocery store.

Tell Me a Story

Directions: Number these sentences from 1 to 5 to show the correct order of the story.

Building a Treehouse

_____ They had a beautiful treehouse!

_____ They got wood and nails.

___1___ Jay and Lisa planned to build a treehouse.

_____ Now, they like to eat lunch in their treehouse.

_____ Lisa and Jay worked in the backyard for three days building the treehouse.

A School Play

_____ Everyone clapped when the curtain closed.

_____ The girl who played Snow White came onto the stage.

_____ All the other school children went to the gym to see the play.

_____ The stage curtain opened.

___1___ The third grade was going to put on a play about Snow White.

House Hunt

Directions: Learning to follow directions is very important. Use the map to find your way to different houses.

1. Color the start house yellow.

2. Go north 2 houses, and east two houses.

3. Go north 2 houses, and west 4 houses.

4. Color the house green.

5. Start at the yellow house.

6. Go east 1 house, and north 3 houses.

7. Go west 3 houses, and south 3 houses.

8. Color the house blue.

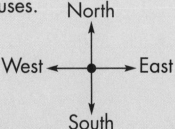

Super Salad

Following directions means doing what the directions say to do. Following directions is an important skill to know. When you are trying to find a new place, build a model airplane or use a recipe, you should follow the directions given.

Directions: Read the following recipe. Then, answer the questions on page 24.

Fruit Salad

1   fresh pineapple
1   cantaloupe
2   bananas
1   cup strawberries
2   oranges
1   pear
1   cup seedless grapes
lemon juice

- Cut the pineapple into chunks.

- Use a small metal scoop to make balls of the cantaloupe.

- Slice the pear, bananas and strawberries.

- Peel the oranges and divide them into sections. Cut each section into bite-sized pieces.

- Dip each piece of fruit in lemon juice, then combine them in a large bowl.

- Cover and chill.

- Pour a fruit dressing of your choice over the chilled fruit, blend well and serve cold.

   Makes 4 large servings.

Super Salad

Directions: Using the recipe on page 23, answer the questions below.

1. How many bananas does this recipe require? _____

2. Does the recipe explain why you
   must dip the fruit in lemon juice? _____

   Why would it be important to do this? _____

   _____

3. Would your fruit salad be as good if you did not cut the
   pineapple or section the oranges? Why or why not?

   _____

   _____

4. Which do you do first?
   (Check one.)

   _____ Pour dressing over the fruit.

   _____ Slice the pear.

   _____ Serve the fruit salad.

5. Which three fruits do you slice?

   _____

   _____

   _____

Shy Giants

Directions: Read about the giant panda. Then, answer the questions.

Giant pandas are among the world's favorite animals. They look like big, cuddly stuffed toys. There are not very many pandas left in the world. You may have to travel a long way to see one.

The only place on Earth where pandas live in the wild is in the bamboo forests of the mountains of China. It is hard to see pandas in the forest because they are very shy. They hide among the many bamboo trees. It also is hard to see pandas because there are so few of them. Scientists think there may be less than 1,000 pandas living in the mountains of China.

1. Write a sentence that tells the main idea of this story:

   _____

   _____

2. What are two reasons that it is hard to see pandas in the wild?

   1) _____

   2) _____

3. How many pandas are believed to be living in the mountains of China?

   _____

A Man of Many Talents

Directions: Read about Thomas Jefferson. Then, answer the questions.

Thomas Jefferson was the third president of the United States. He was also an inventor. That means he created things that had never been made before. Thomas Jefferson had many inventions. He built a chair that rotated in circles. He created a rotating music stand. He also made a walking stick that unfolded into a chair. Thomas Jefferson even invented a new kind of plow for farming.

1. The main idea is: (Circle one.)

   Thomas Jefferson was very busy when he was president.

   Thomas Jefferson was a president and an inventor.

2. What do we call a person who has new ideas and makes things that no one else has made before?

   _____

3. List three of Thomas Jefferson's inventions.

   1) _____

   2) _____

   3) _____

Riding Through History

Directions: Read about the bicycle. Then, answer the questions.

One of the first bicycles was made out of wood. It was created in 1790 by an inventor in France. The first bicycle had no pedals. It looked like a horse on wheels. The person who rode the bicycle had to push it with his/her legs. Pedals weren't invented until nearly 50 years later.

Bikes became quite popular in the United States during the 1890s. Streets and parks were filled with people riding them. But those bicycles were still different from the bikes we ride today. They had heavier tires, and the brakes and lights weren't very good. Bicycling is still very popular in the United States. It is a great form of exercise and a handy means of transportation.

1. Who invented the bicycle? _____

2. What did it look like? _____

_____

3. When did bikes become popular in the United States?

_____

4. Where did people ride bikes? _____

5. How is biking good for you? _____

6. How many years have bikes been popular in the

United States? _____

The Peaceful Pueblos

Directions: Read about the Pueblo Native Americans. Then, answer the questions.

The Pueblo (pooh-eb-low) Native Americans live in the southwestern United States in New Mexico and Arizona. They have lived there for hundreds of years. The Pueblos have always been peaceful Native Americans. They never started wars. They only fought if attacked first.

The Pueblos love to dance. Even their dances are peaceful. They dance to ask the gods for rain or sunshine. They dance for other reasons, too. Sometimes the Pueblos wear masks when they dance.

1. The main idea is: (Circle one.)

    Pueblos are peaceful Native Americans who still live in parts of the United States.

    Pueblo Native Americans never started wars.

2. Do Pueblos like to fight? _____

3. What do the Pueblos like to do? _____

    _____

All About Adobe

Directions: Read about adobe houses. Then, answer the questions.

Pueblo Native Americans live in houses made of clay. They are called *adobe* (ah-doe-bee) *houses*. Adobe is a yellow-colored clay that comes from the ground. The hot sun in New Mexico and Arizona helps dry the clay to make strong bricks. The Pueblos have used adobe to build their homes for many years.

Pueblos use adobe for other purposes, too. The women in the tribes make beautiful pottery out of adobe. While the clay is still damp, they form it into shapes. After they have made the bowls and other containers, they paint them with lovely designs.

1. What is the subject of this story?

   _____

2. Who uses clay to make their houses?

   _____

3. How long have they been building adobe houses?

   _____

4. Why do adobe bricks need to be dried?

   _____

Discover the Details

Directions: Read the story. Then, answer the questions.

Thomas Edison was one of America's greatest inventors. An inventor thinks up new machines and new ways of doing things. Edison was born in Milan, Ohio in 1847. He went to school for only three months. His teacher thought he was not very smart because he asked so many questions.

Edison liked to experiment. He had many wonderful ideas. He invented the light bulb and the phonograph (record player).

Thomas Edison died in 1931, but we still use many of his inventions today.

1. What is an inventor?

_____

_____

_____

2. Where was Thomas Edison born?

_____

3. How long did he go to school?

_____

4. What are two of Edison's inventions?

_____

Panda Life

Directions: Read the story. Then, answer the questions.

Giant pandas do not live in families like people do. The only pandas that live together are mothers and their babies. Newborn pandas are very tiny and helpless. They weigh only five ounces when they are born—about the weight of a stick of butter! They are born with their eyes closed, and they have no teeth.

It takes about three years for a panda to grow up. When full grown, a giant panda weighs about 300 pounds and is five to six feet tall. Once a panda is grown up, it leaves its mother and goes off to live by itself.

1. What pandas live together?

   _____

2. How much do pandas weigh when they are born?

   _____

3. Why do newborn pandas live with their mothers?

   _____

4. When is a panda full grown?

   _____

Seeing Hsing-Hsing

Inference is using logic to figure out what is not directly told.

Directions: Read the story. Then, answer the questions.

In the past, many thousands of people went to the National Zoo each year to see Hsing-Hsing, the panda. Sometimes, there were as many as 1,000 visitors in one hour! Like all pandas, Hsing-Hsing spent most of his time sleeping. Because pandas are so rare, most people think it is exciting to see even a sleeping panda!

1. Popular means well-liked. Do you think giant pandas are popular?

_____

2. What clue do you have that pandas are popular?

_____

_____

3. What did most visitors see Hsing-Hsing doing?

_____

Got the Message?

Directions: Read the messages on the memo board. Then, answer the questions.

1. What kind of lesson does Katie have?

   _____

2. What time is Amy's birthday party? _____

3. What kind of appointment does Jeff have on

   September 3rd?_____

4. Who goes to choir practice? _____

5. Where is Dad's meeting?

   _____

All in Order

Dictionaries contain meanings and pronunciations of words. The words in a dictionary are listed in alphabetical order. Guide words appear at the top of each dictionary page. They help us know at a glance what words are on each page.

Directions: Place the words in alphabetical order.

apple	dog	crab	ear
book	atlas	cake	frog
egg	drip	coat	crib

Did You Hear the News?

A newspaper has many parts. Some of the parts of a newspaper are:

- banner — the name of the paper

- lead story — the top news item

- caption — sentences under the picture which give information about the picture

- sports — scores and information on current sports events

- comics — drawings that tell funny stories

- editorial — an article by the editor expressing an opinion about something

- ads — paid advertisements

- weather — information about the weather

- advice column — letters from readers asking for help with a problem

- movie guides — a list of movies and movie times

- obituary — information about people who have died

Directions: Match the newspaper sections below with their definitions.

banner	an article by the editor
lead story	sentences under pictures
caption	movies and movie times
editorial	the name of the paper
movies	information about people who have died
obituary	the top news item

Right on Schedule!

Here is a schedule for the day's activities at Camp Do-A-Lot. Amira and Jessie need help to decide what they will do on their last day.

Directions: Use this schedule to answer the questions on page 37.

CAMP DO-A-LOT

Saturday

Breakfast	6:30 A.M.	Dining Hall
Archery	7:30 A.M.	Field behind the Hall
Canoeing	7:30 A.M.	Blue Bottom Lake
Landscape Painting	7:30 A.M.	Rainbow Craft Shed
Horseback Riding	8:45 A.M.	Red Barn
Landscape Painting	8:45 A.M.	Rainbow Craft Shed
Scavenger Hunt	8:45 A.M.	Dining Hall
Cabin Clean-up	10:45 A.M.	Assigned Cabins
Lunch	11:45 A.M.	Dining Hall
Canoeing	1:00 P.M.	Blue Bottom Lake
Archery	1:00 P.M.	Field behind the Hall
Scavenger Hunt	1:00 P.M.	Dining Hall
Awards Ceremony	2:45 P.M.	Outdoor Theater
Dismissal	3:30 P.M.	

Right on Schedule!

Directions: Use the schedule of activities on page 36 to answer the questions.

1. Where do Amira and Jessie need to go to take part in archery?

   _____

2. Both girls want to go canoeing. What are the two times that canoeing is offered?

   _____ and _____

3. Amira and Jessie love to go on scavenger hunts. They agree to go on the hunt at 1:00 P.M. When will they have to go canoeing?

   _____

4. Only one activity on the last day of camp takes place at the Outdoor Theater. What is it?

   _____

Pretend you are at Camp Do-A-Lot with Amira and Jessie. On the line next to each time, write which activity you would choose to do.

7:30 A.M. _____

8:45 A.M. _____

1:00 P.M. _____

Get Real!

Something that is **real** could actually happen. Something that is **fantasy** is not real. It could not happen.

Examples: Real: Dogs can bark.
　　　　　Fantasy: Dogs can fly.

Directions: Look at the sentences below. Write **real** or **fantasy** next to each sentence.

1. My cat can talk to me. _____

2. Witches ride brooms and cast spells. _____

3. Dad can mow the lawn. _____

4. I ride a magic carpet to school. _____

5. I have a man-eating tree. _____

6. My sandbox has toys in it. _____

7. Mom can bake chocolate chip cookies. _____

8. Mark's garden has tomatoes and corn in it. _____

Write your own real sentence.

_____

Write your own fantasy sentence.

_____

Introducing Idioms

Idioms are a colorful way of saying something ordinary. The words in idioms do not mean exactly what they say.

Directions: Read the idioms listed below. Draw a picture of the literal meaning. Then, match the idiom to its correct meaning.

Jump on the bandwagon! ●

● She doesn't eat very much.

She eats like a bird. ●

● Keep the secret.

Don't cry over spilled milk! ●

● Get involved!

Don't let the cat out of the bag! ●

● Don't worry about things that have already happened.

You are the apple of my eye. ●

● I think you are special.

All in the Family

Analogies compare how things are related to each other.

Directions: Complete the other analogies.

Example: Finger is to **hand** as **toe** is to **foot**.

1. Apple is to tree   as   flower is to _____.

2. Tire is to car   as   wheel is to _____.

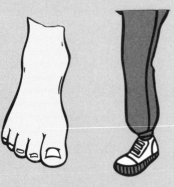  

3. Foot is to leg   as   hand is to _____.

40

Awesome Analogies

Directions: Complete each analogy using a word from the box. The first one has been done for you.

week   bottom   month   tiny   sentence   out   eye

1. **Up** is to **down**   as

   in is to _____.

2. **Minute** is to **hour**   as

   day is to _____.

3. **Month** is to **year**   as

   week is to _____.

4. **Over** is to **under**   as

   top is to _____.

5. **Big** is to **little**   as

   giant is to _____.

6. **Sound** is to **ear**   as

   sight is to _____.

7. **Page** is to **book**   as

   word is to _____.

In the Garden

Directions: Write each word from the box in the correct category.

robin	elm	buckeye	willow
sunflower	bluejay	canary	oak
rose	wren	tulip	morning glory

Trees

_____

_____

_____

_____

Birds

_____

_____

_____

_____

Flowers

_____

_____

_____

_____

Find the Kind

Directions: Write the word from the word box that tells what kinds of things are in each sentence.

birds	men	toys	states
animals	insects	flowers	letters

1. A father, uncle and king are all _____.

2. Fred has a wagon, puzzles and blocks. These are all

   _____.

3. Iowa, Ohio and Maine are all _____.

4. A robin, woodpecker and canary all have wings. They

   are kinds of _____.

5. Squirrels, rabbits and foxes all have tails and are kinds

   of _____.

6. Roses, daisies and violets smell sweet. These are kinds

   of _____.

7. A, B, C and D are all _____.
   You use them to spell words.

8. Bees, ladybugs and beetles are kinds of

   _____.

Bookshelf Basics

A **fiction** book is a book about things that are made up or not true. Fantasy books are fiction. A **nonfiction** book is about things that have really happened. Books can be classified into more types:

Mystery – books that have clues that lead to solving a problem or mystery

Biography – book about a real person's life

Poetry – a collection of poems, which may or may not rhyme

Fantasy – books about things that cannot really happen

Sports – books about different sports or sport figures

Travel – books about going to other places

Directions: Write mystery, biography, poetry, fantasy, sports or travel next to each title.

The Life of Helen Keller _____

Let's Go to Mexico! _____

The Case of the Missing Doll _____

How to Play Golf _____

Turtle Soup and Other Poems _____

Fred's Flying Saucer _____

Real or Fantasy?

Directions: Read the paragraphs below. Determine whether each paragraph is fiction or nonfiction. Circle the letter **F** for fiction or the letter **N** for nonfiction.

Megan and Mariah skipped out to the playground. They enjoyed playing together at recess. Today, it was Mariah's turn to choose what they would do first. To Megan's surprise, Mariah asked, "What do you want to do, Megan? I'm going to let you pick since it's your birthday!" **F N**

It is easy to tell an insect from a spider. An insect has three body parts and six legs. A spider has eight legs and no wings. Of course, if you see the creature spinning a web, you will know what it is. An insect wouldn't want to get too close to the web or it would be stuck. It might become dinner! **F N**

My name is Lee Chang, and I live in a country that you call China. My home is on the other side of the world from yours. When the sun is rising in my country, it is setting in yours. When it is day at your home, it is night at mine. **F N**

Author ABCs

Ms. Ling, the school librarian, needs help shelving books. Fiction titles are arranged in alphabetical order by the author's last name. Ms. Ling has done the first set for you.

__3__ Silverstein, Shel

__1__ Bridwell, Norman

__2__ Farley, Walter

Directions: Number the following groups of authors in alphabetical order.

_____ Bemelmans, Ludwig   _____ Perkins, Al

_____ Stein, R.L.   _____ Dobbs, Rose

_____ Sawyer, Ruth   _____ Baldwin, James

_____ Baum, L. Frank   _____ Kipling, Rudyard

The content of some books is also arranged alphabetically.

Directions: Circle the books that are arranged in alphabetical order.

T.V. guide	dictionary	encyclopedia	novel
almanac	science book	Yellow Pages	catalog

Write the books you circled in alphabetical order.

1. _____

2. _____

3. _____

Pick a Periodical

Libraries also have periodicals such as magazines and newspapers. They are called **periodicals** because they are printed regularly within a set period of time. There are many kinds of magazines. Some discuss the news. Others cover fitness, cats or other topics of special interest. Almost every city or town has a newspaper. Newspapers usually are printed daily, weekly or even monthly. Newspapers cover what is happening in your town and in the world. They usually include sections on sports and entertainment. They present a lot of information.

Directions: Follow the instructions.

1. Choose an interesting magazine. What is the name of

   the magazine? _____
   List the titles of three articles in the magazine.

   _____

   _____

   _____

2. Now, look at a newspaper. What is the name of the

   newspaper? _____
   The title of a newspaper story is called a headline. What are some of the headlines in your local newspaper?

   _____

   _____

   _____

City Kids

Directions: Look for similarities and differences in the following paragraphs. Then, answer the questions.

Phong and Chris both live in the city. They live in the same apartment building and go to the same school. Phong and Chris sometimes walk to school together. If it is raining or storming, Phong's dad drives them to school on his way to work. In the summer, they spend a lot of time at the park across the street from their building.

Phong lives in Apartment 12-A with his little sister and mom and dad. He has a collection of model race cars that he put together with his dad's help. He even has a bookshelf full of books about race cars and race car drivers.

Chris has a big family. He has two older brothers and one older sister. When Chris has time to do anything he wants, he gets out his butterfly collection. He notes the place he found each specimen and the day he found it. He also likes to play with puzzles.

1. Compare Phong and Chris. List at least three similarities.

_____

_____

_____

2. Contrast Phong and Chris. List two differences.

_____

_____

_____

Taking Flight

Directions: List the similarities and differences you find below on a chart called a **Venn diagram**. This kind of chart shows comparisons and contrasts.

Butterflies and moths belong to the same group of insects. They both have two pairs of wings. Their wings are covered with tiny scales. Both butterflies and moths undergo metamorphosis, or a change, in their lives. They begin their lives as caterpillars.

Butterflies and moths are different in some ways. Butterflies usually fly during the day, but moths generally fly at night. Most butterflies have slender, hairless bodies; most moths have plump, furry bodies. When butterflies land, they hold their wings together straight over their bodies. When moths land, they spread their wings out flat.

1. List three ways that butterflies and moths are alike.

   _____

   _____

   _____

2. List three ways that butterflies and moths are different.

   _____

   _____

   _____

3. Combine your answers from questions 1 and 2 into a Venn diagram. Write the differences in the circle labeled for each insect. Write the similarities in the intersecting part.

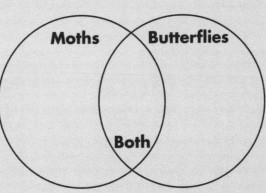

For a Good Cause

A **cause** is the reason for an event. An **effect** is what happens as a result of a cause.

Directions: Circle the cause and underline the effect in each sentence. They may be in any order. The first one has been done for you.

1. (The truck hit an icy patch) and <u>skidded off the road.</u>

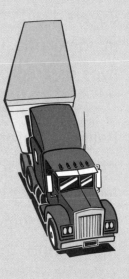

2. When the door slammed shut, the baby woke up crying.

3. Our soccer game was cancelled when it began to storm.

4. Dad and Mom are adding a room onto the house since our family is growing.

5. Our car ran out of gas on the way to town, so we had to walk.

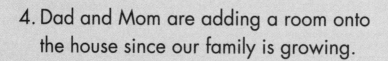

6. The home run in the ninth inning helped our team win the game.

7. We had to climb the stairs because the elevator was broken.

Searching for Clues

Cause and effect sentences often use clue words to show the relationship between two events. Common clue words are **because**, **so**, **when** and **since**.

Directions: Read the sentences below. Circle each clue word. The first one has been done for you.

1. I'll help you clean your room, so we can go out to play sooner.

2. Because of the heavy snowfall, school was closed today.

3. She was not smiling, so her mother wanted her school pictures taken again.

4. Mrs. Wilderman came to school with crutches today, because she had a skating accident.

5. When the team began making too many mistakes at practice, the coach told them to take a break.

Action . . . Reaction!

Directions: Draw a line to match each phrase to form a logical cause and effect sentence.

1. Dad gets paid today, so

2. When the electricity went out,

3. Courtney can't spend the night

4. Our front window shattered

because she is sick.

we're going out for dinner.

we grabbed the flashlights.

when the baseball hit it.

Directions: Read each sentence beginning. Choose an ending from the box that makes sense. Write the correct letter on the line.

1. Her arm was in a cast, because _____

2. They are building a new house on our street, so _____

3. Since I'd always wanted a puppy, _____

4. I had to renew my library book, _____

A. we all went down to watch.

B. since I hadn't finished it.

C. she fell when she was skating.

D. Mom gave me one for my birthday.

Get Ready For Robots

Directions: Read the story. Then, answer the questions.

There are many different kinds of robots. One special kind of robot takes the place of people in guiding airplanes and ships. They are called "automatic pilots." These robots are really computers programmed to do just one special job. They have the information to control the speed and direction of the plane or ship.

Robots are used for many jobs in which a person can't get too close because of danger, such as in exploding a bomb. Robots can be controlled from a distance. This is called "remote control." These robots are very important in studying space. In the future, robots will be used to work on space stations and on other planets.

1. The main idea of this story is:

   _____

   _____

2. Why are robots good in dangerous jobs?

   _____

3. What is "remote control"?

   _____

4. What will robots be used for in the future?

   _____

5. What would you have a robot do for you?

   _____

Swamp Creatures

Brontosaurus dinosaurs lived in the swamps. Swamps are water areas where many plants grow. Here are the names of the other kinds of dinosaurs that lived in the swamps. Diplodocus (dip-low-dock-us), Brachiosaurus (bracky-o-saur-us) and Cetiosaurus (set-e-o-saur-us). These dinosaurs had small heads and small brains. They weighed 20 tons or more. They grew to be 60 feet long! These animals did not need to have sharp teeth.

Directions: Answer these questions about Brontosaurus and other big dinosaurs.

1. These big dinosaurs did not have sharp teeth. What did they eat?

    _____

2. Why were swamps a good place for these big dinosaurs to live?

    _____

    _____

3. These big dinosaurs had small brains. Do you think they were smart? Why?

    _____

    _____

4. Name the three kinds of dinosaurs that lived in swamps.

    _____

    _____

The Frilly Lizard

Triceratops was one of the last dinosaurs to develop. It lived in the Cretaceous (kre-tay-shus) period of history. It was in this time that the dinosaurs became extinct. Triceratops means "three-horned lizard." It was a strong dinosaur and able to defend itself well since it lived during the same time period as Tyrannosaurus Rex.

Triceratops was a plant-eating dinosaur. Its body was 20 feet long, and its head, including the three horns and bony "frill," was another $6\frac{1}{2}$ feet.

Directions: Answer these questions about Triceratops.

1. Dinosaurs became extinct during the

   _____ period of history.

2. What does **Triceratops** mean?

   _____

3. What information above tells you that Triceratops was able to defend itself?

   _____

   _____

Dino Tracks

Dinosaurs roamed the Earth for 125 million years. Can you imagine that much time? About 40 years ago, some people found fossils of dinosaur tracks in Connecticut. Fossils are rocks that hold the hardened bones, eggs and footprints of animals that lived long ago. The fossil tracks showed that many dinosaurs walked together in herds. The fossils showed more than 2,000 dinosaur tracks!

Directions: Answer these questions about fossils.

1. What did the people find in the fossils?

   _____

2. In what state were the fossils found?

   _____

3. How many tracks were in the fossils?

   _____

4. What did the tracks show?

   _____

5. How long did dinosaurs roam the Earth?

   _____

Model Mania

Some people can build models of dinosaurs. The models are fakes, of course. But they are life-size and they look real! The people who build them must know the dinosaur inside and out. First, they build a skeleton. Then, they cover it with fake "skin." Then, they paint it. Some models have motors in them. The motors can make the dinosaur's head or tail move. Have you ever seen a life-size model of a dinosaur?

Directions: Answer these questions about dinosaur models.

1. Circle the main idea:

   Some models of dinosaurs have motors in them.

   Some people can build life-size models of dinosaurs that look real.

2. What do the motors in model dinosaurs do?

   _____

   _____

3. What is the first step in making a model dinosaur?

   _____

   _____

4. Why do dinosaur models look real?

   _____

   _____

Growing Up . . . and Up and Up!

Kareem Abdul-Jabbar grew up to be more than 7 feet tall! Kareem's father and mother were both very tall. When he was 9 years old, Kareem was already 5 feet 4 inches tall. Kareem was raised in New York City. He went to Power Memorial High School and played basketball on that team. He went to college at UCLA. He played basketball in college, too. At UCLA, Kareem's team lost only two games in 3 years! After college, Kareem made his living playing basketball.

Directions: Answer these questions about Kareem Abdul-Jabbar.

1. Who is the story about?

    _____

2. For what is this athlete famous?

    _____

3. When did Kareem reach the height of 5 feet 4 inches?

    _____

4. Where did Kareem go to college?

    _____

5. Why did Kareem grow so tall?

    _____

    _____

Small but Mighty

Mary Lou Retton became the first U.S. woman to win Olympic gold in gymnastics. She accomplished this at the 1984 Olympics held in Los Angeles, when she was 16 years old. "Small but mighty" would certainly describe this gymnast.

She was the youngest of five children—all good athletes. She grew up in Fairmont, West Virginia, and began her gymnastic training at the age of 7.

Most women gymnasts are graceful, but Mary Lou helped open up the field of gymnastics to strong, athletic women. Mary Lou was 4 feet 10 inches tall and weighed a mere 95 pounds!

Directions: Answer these questions about Mary Lou Retton.

1. Circle the main idea:

   Mary Lou loved performing.

   Mary Lou is a famous Olympic gymnast.

2. She was born in _____.

3. At what age did she begin her gymnastics training?

   _____

4. Mary Lou won a gold medal when she was _____ years old.

Journey to a New Frontier

In 1801, President Thomas Jefferson chose an army officer named Meriwether Lewis to lead an expedition through our country's "new frontier." He knew Lewis would not be able to make the journey by himself, so he chose William Clark to travel with him. The two men had known each other in the army. They decided to be co-leaders of the expedition.

The two men and a group of about 45 others made the trip from the state of Missouri, across the Rocky Mountains all the way to the Pacific Coast. They were careful in choosing the men who would travel with them. They wanted men who were strong and knew a lot about the wilderness. It was also important that they knew some of the Native American languages.

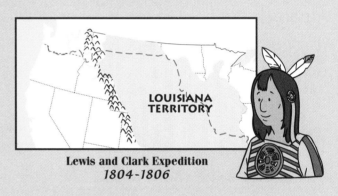

Lewis and Clark Expedition
1804-1806

Directions: Answer these questions about Lewis and Clark.

1. Which president wanted an expedition through the "new frontier"?

   _____

2. Look at a United States map or a globe. In what direction did Lewis and Clark travel? (Circle one.)

   north   south   east   west

3. About how many people made up the entire expedition, including Lewis and Clark?

   _____

Trials of the Trail

Lewis and Clark and their men had seen large grizzly bears as they traveled through the West. They were thankful they had their weapons with them. But meeting the grizzlies was not the hardest part of the journey. It was also hard to cross the Rocky Mountains.
It took the explorers and their "party" a month to make this part of their trip. The friendly Shoshone tribe was very helpful in telling them how they could cross the mountains.

There were many reasons why this part of the trip was difficult. The steep, narrow pathways sometimes caused the horses to fall over the cliffs to their deaths. Many times the men had to lead the horses. There were also fewer wild animals for the men to hunt for food.

Directions: Answer these questions about the hardships of the expedition.

1. What was the hardest part of the trip?

   _____

2. Lewis and Clark got help from which friendly Native American tribe?

   _____

3. What word in the story means "a group of people traveling together"?

   _____

4. What caused some of the horses to fall to their deaths?

   _____

The Thief of Sherwood Forest

Long ago in England there lived a man named Robin Hood. Robin lived with a group of other men in the woods. These woods were called Sherwood Forest.

Robin Hood was a thief—a different kind of thief. He stole from the rich and gave what he stole to the poor. Poor people did not need to worry about going into Sherwood Forest. In fact, Robin Hood often gave them money. Rich people were told to beware. If you were rich, would you stay out of Sherwood Forest?

Directions: Answer these questions about Robin Hood.

1. What was the name of the woods where Robin Hood live?

   _____

2. What did Robin Hood do for a living?

   _____

3. What was different about Robin Hood?

   _____

4. Did poor people worry about going into Sherwood Forest? Why or why not?

   _____

5. Do you think rich people worried about going into Sherwood Forest? Why?

   _____

Robin Hood and the King

Everyone in England knew about Robin Hood. The king was mad! He did not want a thief to be a hero. He sent his men to Sherwood Forest to catch Robin Hood. But they could not catch him. Robin Hood outsmarted the king's men every time!

One day, Robin Hood sent a message to the king. The message said, "Come with five brave men. We will see who is stronger." The king decided to fool Robin Hood. He wanted to see if what people said about Robin Hood was true. The king dressed as a monk. A monk is a poor man who serves God. Then, he went to Sherwood Forest to see Robin Hood.

Directions: Circle the correct answer to these questions about the king's meeting with Robin Hood.

1. If the stories about Robin Hood were true, what happened when the king met Robin Hood?

    Robin Hood robbed the king and took all his money.

    Robin Hood helped the king because he thought he was a poor man.

2. Why didn't the king want Robin Hood to know who he was?

    He was afraid of Robin Hood.

    He wanted to find out what Robin Hood was really like.

3. Why couldn't the king's men find Robin Hood?

    Robin Hood outsmarted them.

    They didn't look in Sherwood Forest.

Robin Hood and the King

The king liked Robin Hood. He said, "Here is a man who likes a good joke." He told Robin Hood who he really was. Robin Hood was not mad. He laughed and laughed. The king invited Robin Hood to come and live in the castle. The castle was 20 miles away. Robin had to walk south, cross a river and make two left turns to get there. He stayed inside the castle grounds for a year and a day.

Then, Robin grew restless and asked the king for permission to leave. The king did not want him to go. He said Robin Hood could visit Sherwood Forest for only one week. Robin said he missed his men but promised to return. The king knew Robin Hood never broke his promises.

Directions: Answer these questions about Robin Hood and the king.

1. Do you think Robin Hood returned to the castle? _____

2. Why do you think Robin Hood laughed when the king told him the truth?

   _____

3. Give directions from Sherwood Forest to the king's castle.

   _____

   _____

4. Circle the main idea:

   The king liked Robin Hood, but Robin missed his life in Sherwood Forest.

   Robin Hood thought the castle was boring.

Crazy for Catnip!

Do you have a cat? Do you have catnip growing around your home? If you don't know, your cat probably does. Cats love the catnip plant and can be seen rolling around in it. Some cat toys have catnip inside them because cats love it so much.

People can enjoy catnip, too. Some people make catnip tea with the leaves of the plant. It is like the mint with which people make tea.

Another refreshing drink can be made with the berries of the sumac bush or tree. Native Americans would pick the red berries, crush them and add water to make a thirst-quenching drink. The berries were sour, but they must have believed that the cool, tart drink was refreshing. Does this remind you of lemonade?

Directions: Answer these questions about unusual plants.

1. What is the main idea of the first two paragraphs above?

   _____

   _____

2. Write two ways cats show that they love catnip.

   1) _____

   2) _____

3. How can people use catnip?

   _____

   _____

The Greenest Place on Earth

The soil in rainforests is very dark and rich. The trees and plants that grow there are very green. People who have seen one say a rainforest is "the greenest place on Earth." Why? Because it rains a lot. With so much rain, the plants stay very green. The earth stays very wet. Rainforests cover only 6 percent of the Earth. But they are home to 66 percent of all the different kinds of plants and animals on Earth! Today, rainforests are threatened by such things as acid rain from factory smoke emissions around the world and from farm expansion. Farmers living near rainforests cut down many trees each year to clear the land for farming.

Directions: Answer these questions about rainforests.

1. What do the plants and trees in a rainforest look like?

   _____

2. What is the soil like in a rainforest?

   _____

3. How much of the Earth is covered by rainforests?

   _____

4. What percentage of the Earth's plants and animals live there?

   _____

The Kinkajou

If you have ever seen a raccoon holding its food by its "hands" and carefully eating it, you would have an idea of how the kinkajou (king-kuh-joo) eats. This animal of the rainforest is a "cousin" of the raccoon. Unlike its North American cousin, though, it is a golden-brown color.

The kinkajou's head and body are 17 to 22 inches long. The long tail of the kinkajou comes in handy for hanging around its neighborhood! It weighs very little—about 5 pounds. (You may have a 5-pound bag of sugar or flour in your kitchen to help you get an idea of the kinkajou's weight.)

This rainforest animal eats a variety of things. It enjoys nectar from the many rainforest flowers, insects, fruit, honey, birds and other small animals. Because it lives mostly in the trees, the kinkajou has a ready supply of food.

Directions: Answer these questions about the kinkajou.

1. The kinkajou is a "cousin" to the _____.

2. Do you weigh more or less than the kinkajou? _____

3. Write three things the kinkajou eats.

    1) _____

    2) _____

    3) _____

A Trip to the Rainforest

Many people travel to the rainforest each year. Some go by car, some go by train and some go by school bus! You don't even need a passport—the only thing you need is a field-trip permission slip.

If you are lucky enough to live in the Cleveland, Ohio area, you might get to take a class trip to the rainforest there. It is next to the Cleveland Zoo. This "rainforest" is a building that contains all the sights, sounds, smells and temperatures of the real rainforest. You will get to see many of the animals, big and small, that you could see if you went to Central or South America. The plants that grow there also grow in the rainforest. It is an interesting way to get an idea of what life is like in that part of the world!

Directions: Answer these questions about visiting the "rainforest."

1. If you lived in northern Ohio, name three ways you could get to the "rainforest."

   _____

2. In this "rainforest" you can see _____ and

   _____ that are found in the real rainforest.

3. Do you think it would be hot or cold in this "rainforest" building?

   hot   cold

4. The real rainforest is located in both _____

   _____ and _____.

Not Just Any Cat

The jaguar weighs between 100 and 250 pounds. It can be as long as 6 feet! This is not your ordinary house cat!

One strange feature of the jaguar is its living arrangements. The jaguar has its own territory. No other jaguar lives in its "home range." It would be very unusual for one jaguar to meet another in the rainforest. One way they mark their territory is by scratching trees.

Have you ever seen your pet cat hide in the grass and carefully and quietly sneak up on an unsuspecting grasshopper or mouse? Like its gentler, smaller "cousin," the jaguar stalks its prey in the high grass. It likes to eat small animals, such as rodents, but can attack and kill larger animals such as tapirs, deer and cattle. It is good at catching fish as well.

Directions: Answer these questions about the jaguar.

1. The jaguar lives:

   a. in large groups

   b. alone

   c. under water

2. This large cat marks its territory by:

   a. black marker

   b. roaring

   c. scratching trees

3. What does the jaguar eat?

_____

4. How much does it weigh?

_____

Out of This World

There are eight planets in our solar system. All of them circle the Sun. The planet closest to the Sun is named Mercury. The Romans said Mercury was the messenger of the gods. The second planet from the Sun is named Venus. Venus shines the brightest. Venus was the Roman goddess of beauty. Earth is the third planet from the Sun. It is about the same size as Venus. After Earth is Mars, which is named after the Roman god of war. The other four planets are Jupiter, Saturn, Uranus, and Neptune. They, too, are named after Roman gods.

Directions: Answer these questions about our solar system.

1. How many planets are in our solar system?

   _____

2. What do the planets circle?

   _____

3. What are the planets named after?

   _____

4. Which planet is closest to the Sun?

   _____

5. Which planet is about the same size as Earth?

   _____

A Visit to Venus

For many years, no one knew much about Venus. When people looked through telescopes, they could not see past Venus' clouds. Long ago, people thought the clouds covered living things. Spacecraft radar has shown this is not true. Venus is too hot for life to exist. The temperature on Venus is about 900 degrees! Remember how hot you were the last time it was 90 degrees? Now imagine it being 10 times hotter. Nothing could exist in that heat. It is also very dry on Venus. For life to exist, water must be present. Because of the heat and dryness, we know there are no people, plants or other life on Venus.

Directions: Answer these questions about Venus.

1. Circle the main idea:

   We cannot see past Venus' clouds to know what the planet is like.

   Spacecraft radar shows it is too hot and dry for life to exist on Venus.

2. What is the temperature on Venus? _____

3. This temperature is how many times hotter than a hot day on Earth?

   6 times hotter

   10 times hotter

4. In the past, why did people think life might exist on Venus?

   _____

   _____

Welcome to Earth!

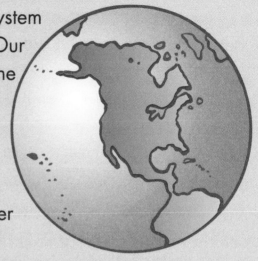

One planet in our solar system certainly supports life—Earth. Our planet is the third planet from the Sun and takes 365 days, or 1 year, to orbit the Sun. This rotation makes it possible for most of our planet to have four seasons—winter, spring, summer and fall.

Besides being able to support life, our planet is unique in another way—Earth is 75% covered by water. No other planet has that much, if any, liquid on its surface. This liquid and its evaporation help provide the cloud cover and our climate patterns.

Earth has one natural satellite—the Moon. Scientists and other experts all over the world have created and sent into orbit other satellites used for a variety of purposes—communication, weather forecasting, and so on.

Directions: Answer these questions about Earth.

1. How much of Earth is covered by water? _____

2. The Moon is a _____ of Earth.

3. How long does it take Earth to orbit the Sun?

_____

4. How does water make Earth the "living planet"?

_____

_____

Making It to the Moon

Our moon is not the only moon in the solar system. Some other planets have moons also. Saturn has 10 moons! Our moon is Earth's closest neighbor in the solar system. Sometimes our moon is 225,727 miles away. Other times, it is 252,002 miles away. Why? Because the Moon revolves around Earth. It does not go around Earth in a perfect circle. So, sometimes its path takes it further away from our planet.

When our astronauts visited the Moon, they found dusty plains, high mountains and huge craters. There is no air or water on the Moon. That is why life cannot exist there. The astronauts had to wear space suits to protect their skin from the bright Sun. They had to take their own air to breathe. They had to take their own food and water.

Directions: Answer these questions about the Moon.

1. Circle the main idea:

   The Moon travels around Earth, and the astronauts visited the Moon.

   Astronauts found that the Moon—Earth's closest neighbor—has no air or water and cannot support life.

2. Write three things our astronauts found on the Moon.

   1) _____ 2) _____ 3) _____

3. Make a list of what to take on a trip to the Moon.

   _____

   _____

Bag of Bones

Are you scared of skeletons? You shouldn't be. There is a skeleton inside of you! The skeleton is made up of all the bones in your body. These 206 bones give you your shape. They also protect your heart and everything else inside. Your bones come in many sizes. Some are short. Some are long. Some are rounded. Some are very tiny. The outside of your bones looks solid. Inside, they are filled with a soft material called marrow. This is what keeps your bones alive. Red blood cells and most white blood cells are made here. These cells help feed the body and fight disease.

Directions: Answer these questions about your bones.

1. Do you think your leg bone is short, long or rounded?

   _____

2. Do you think the bones in your head are short, long or rounded?

   _____

3. What is the size of the bones in your fingers?

   _____

4. What is the "something soft" inside your bones?

   _____

Making Muscles

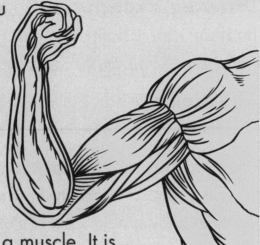

Can you make a fist? You could not do this without muscles. You need muscles to make your body move. You have muscles everywhere. There are muscles in your legs. There are even muscles in your tongue!

Remember, your heart is a muscle. It is called an "involuntary muscle" because it works without help from you. Your stomach muscles are also involuntary. You don't need to tell your stomach to digest food. Other muscles are called "voluntary muscles." You must tell these muscles to move. Most voluntary muscles are hooked to bones. When the muscles squeeze, they cause the bone to move. Without your muscles, you would be nothing but a "bag of bones"!

Directions: Answer these questions about your muscles.

1. What are involuntary muscles?

   _____

2. What are voluntary muscles?

   _____

3. Which muscles are usually hooked to bones?

   _____

4. What causes bones to move?

   _____

Get a Clue!

Drawing a conclusion means to use clues to make a final decision about something. To draw a conclusion, you must read carefully.

Directions: Read each story carefully. Use the clues given to draw a conclusion about the story.

The boy and girl took turns pushing the shopping cart. They went up and down the aisles. Each time they stopped the cart, they would look at things on the shelf and decide what they needed. Jody asked her older brother, "Will I need a box of 48 crayons in Mrs. Charles' class?"

"Yes, I think so," he answered. Then, he turned to their mother and said, "I need some new notebooks. Can I get some?"

1. Where are they? _____

2. What are they doing there? _____

3. How do you know? Write at least two clue words that

helped you. _____

Eric and Randy held on tight. They looked around them and saw that they were not the only ones holding on. The car moved slowly upward. As they turned and looked over the side, they noticed that the people far below them seemed to be getting smaller and smaller. "Hey, Eric, did I tell you this is my first time on one of these?" asked Randy. As they started down the hill at a frightening speed, Randy screamed, "And it may be my last!"

1. Where are they? _____

2. How do you know? Write at least two clue words that

helped you. _____

Mrs. Posy's Roses

Directions: Read the story. Then, answer the questions.

Mrs. Posy plants roses everywhere. She plants yellow roses near her front porch. She plants red roses near the back door. There are also pink roses and white roses in her yard. Every time the postal carrier comes to her house, he sneezes. "You should not plant so many flowers," he tells Mrs. Posy. Mrs. Posy just smiles.

1. What are Mrs. Posy's favorite flowers? _____

2. Why do you think the postal carrier tells Mrs. Posy, "You should not plant so many flowers"?

   _____

   _____

3. Why does Mrs. Posy smile?

   _____

   _____

What's Hiding?

Directions: Read about caterpillars. Then, answer the questions.

Some people do not like caterpillars. Caterpillars look like fuzzy worms. They have many legs and they creep and crawl on trees and leaves. But a caterpillar is really the beginning of something else. After the caterpillar is very large, it spins a cocoon. It stays inside the cocoon for a few months. When the cocoon opens, something else is inside. It is very beautiful. It flies away.

1. Why would people dislike caterpillars? _____

_____

2. What happens while the caterpillar is in the cocoon?

_____

_____

3. When does the cocoon open? _____

_____

4. What comes out of the cocoon? _____

_____

English

Egg-cellent!

Directions: Alphabetical order is putting words in the order in which they appear in the alphabet. Put the eggs in alphabetical order. The first and last words are done for you.

1. basket _____

6. _____

2. _____

7. _____

11. _____

3. _____

8. _____

12. _____

15. _____

18. _____

4. _____

9. _____

13. _____

16. _____

19. _____

5. _____

10. _____

14. _____

17. _____

20. zero

Let's Start with ABC

Alphabetical order is the order in which letters come in the alphabet.

Directions: Write the words in alphabetical order. If the first letter is the same, use the second letter of each word to decide which word comes first. If the second letter is also the same, look at the third letter of each word to decide.

Example: w(i)sh   w(a)sp   w(o)n't

1. w**a**sp

2. w**i**sh

3. w**o**n't

bench   flag   bowl   egg   nod   neat

1. _____   1. _____

2. _____   2. _____

3. _____   3. _____

dog   dart   drag   skipped   stairs   stones

1. _____   1. _____

2. _____   2. _____

3. _____   3. _____

Only Opposites

An antonym is a word that means the opposite of another word.

Examples:

child   adult

hot   cold

Directions: Match the words that have opposite meanings. Draw a line between each pair of antonyms.

thaw   same

huge   sad

crying   friend

happy   open

enemy   freeze

asleep   thin

closed   hide

fat   tiny

seek   awake

different   laughing

Ask Me About Antonyms

Antonyms are words that are opposites.

Example: **hairy**   **bald**

Directions: Choose a word from the box to complete each sentence below.

open	right	light	full	below
hard	clean	quiet	old	nice

Example:

My car was **dirty**, but now it's **clean**.

1. Sometimes my cat is naughty, and sometimes

   she's _____.

2. The sign said, "Closed," but the door

   was _____.

3. Is the glass half empty or half _____?

4. I bought new shoes, but I like my _____ ones better.

5. Skating is easy for me, but _____ for my brother.

6. The sky is dark at night and _____ during the day.

7. I like a noisy house, but my mother likes a

   _____ one.

8. My friend says I'm wrong, but I say

   I'm _____.

So Many Synonyms!

Synonyms are words with nearly the same meaning.

Directions: Draw a line to match each word on the left with its synonym on the right.

infant	hello
forest	coat
bucket	grin
hi	baby
bunny	woods
cheerful	fall
jacket	repair
alike	small
smile	same
autumn	hop
little	skinny
thin	top
jump	rabbit
shirt	pail
fix	happy

Synonym Sense

Directions: Match the pairs of synonyms.

delight •   • discover

speak •   • tidy

lovely •   • start

find •   • talk

nearly •   • joy

neat •   • almost

big •   • beautiful

sad •   • unhappy

begin •   • large

Directions: Read each sentence. Write the synonym pairs from each sentence in the boxes.

1. That unusual clock is a rare antique.

2. I am glad you are so happy!

3. Becky felt unhappy when she heard the sad news.

From Sea to See

Homophones are words that sound the same but are spelled differently and have different meanings.

Example:

sew   sow    so

Directions: Read the sentences and write the correct word in the blanks.

Example:

blue blew She has **blue** eyes.
The wind **blew** the barn down.

eye I He hurt his left _____ playing ball.

_____ like to learn new things.

see sea Can you _____ the winning runner from here?

He goes diving for pearls under the _____.

eight ate The baby _____ the banana.

Li was _____ years old last year.

one won Jill _____ first prize at the science fair.

I am the only _____ in my family with red hair.

two to too My father likes _____ play tennis.

I like to play, _____.

It takes at least _____ people to play.

Hooray for Homophones

Homophones are words that sound the same but have different spellings and meanings.

Directions: Complete each sentence using a word from the box.

blew	night	blue	knight	hour	in
ant	inn	our	aunt	meet	meat

1. A red _____ crawled up the wall.

2. It will be one _____ before we can go back home.

3. Will you _____ us later?

4. We plan to stay at an _____ during our trip.

5. The king had a _____ who fought bravely.

6. The wind _____ so hard that I almost lost my hat.

7. His jacket was _____.

8. My _____ plans to visit us this week.

9. I will come _____ when it gets too cold outside.

10. It was late at _____ when we finally got there.

11. Do you eat red _____.

12. Come over to see _____ new cat.

Know Your Nouns

Common nouns are nouns that name any member of a group of people, places or things, rather than specific people, places or things.

Directions: Read the sentences below and write the common noun found in each sentence.

Example: ___socks___ My socks do not match.

1. _____ The bird could not fly.

2. _____ Ben likes to eat jelly beans.

3. _____ I am going to meet my mother.

4. _____ We will go swimming in the lake tomorrow.

5. _____ I hope the flowers will grow quickly.

6. _____ We colored eggs together.

7. _____ It is easy to ride a bicycle.

8. _____ My cousin is very tall.

9. _____ Ted and Aliyah went fishing in their boat.

10. _____ They won a prize yesterday.

11. _____ She fell down and twisted her ankle.

12. _____ My brother was born today.

Naming Nouns

Proper nouns are names of specific people, places or things. Proper nouns begin with a capital letter.

Directions: Read the sentences below and circle the proper nouns found in each sentence.

Example: (Aunt Frances) gave me a puppy for my birthday.

1. We lived on Jackson Street before we moved to our new house.

2. Angela's birthday party is tomorrow night.

3. We drove through Cheyenne, Wyoming on our way home.

4. Dr. Charles always gives me a treat for not crying.

5. George Washington was our first president.

6. Our class took a field trip to the Johnson Flower Farm.

7. Uncle Jack lives in New York City.

8. Jada and Elizabeth are best friends.

9. We buy doughnuts at the Grayson Bakery.

10. My favorite movie is *E.T.*

11. We flew to Miami, Florida in a plane.

12. We go to Riverfront Stadium to watch the baseball games.

Plenty of Plurals

A **plural** is more than one person, place or thing. We usually add an **s** to show that a noun names more than one. If a noun ends in **x**, **ch**, **sh** or **s**, we add an **es** to the word.

Example: **pizza** **pizzas**

Directions: Write the plural of the words below.

Example: dog + s = dogs   **Example:** peach + es = peaches

cat _____   lunch _____

boot _____   bunch _____

house _____   punch _____

Example: ax + es = axes   **Example:** glass + es = glasses

fox _____   mess _____

tax _____   guess _____

box _____   class _____

Example: dish + es = dishes

bush _____   **walrus**

ash _____

brush _____   **walruses**

Plenty of Plurals

To write the plural forms of words ending in **y**, we change the **y** to **ie** and add **s**.

Example: pony ___ponies___

Directions: Write the plural of each noun on the lines below.

berry _____

cherry _____

bunny _____

penny _____

family _____

candy _____

party _____

Now, write a story using some of the words that end in **y**. Remember to use capital letters and periods.

_____

_____

_____

_____

_____

_____

ENGLISH

Under the Big Top

Possessive nouns tell who or what is the owner of something. With singular nouns, we use an apostrophe **before** the **s**. With plural nouns, we use an apostrophe **after** the **s**.

Example:

singular: one elephant
The **elephant's** dance was wonderful.

plural: more than one elephant
The **elephants'** dance was wonderful.

Directions: Put the apostrophe in the correct place in each bold word. Then, write the word in the blank.

1. The **lions** cage was big.

   _____

2. The **bears** costumes were purple.

   _____

3. One **boys** laughter was very loud.

   _____

4. The **trainers** dogs were dancing about.

   _____

5. The **mans** popcorn was tasty and good.

   _____

6. **Marks** cotton candy was delicious.

   _____

That's Mine!

Directions: Circle the correct possessive noun in each sentence and write it in the blank.

Example: One _____ girl's _____ mother is a teacher.

(girl's)   girls'

1. The _____ tail is long.

    cat's   cats'

2. One _____ baseball bat is aluminum.

    boy's   boys'

3. Both _____ aprons are white.

    waitresses'   waitress's

4. My _____ apple pie is the best!

    grandmother's   grandmothers'

5. My five _____ uniforms are dirty.

    brother's   brothers'

6. The _____ doll is pretty.

    child's   childs'

Pronoun Power!

Pronouns are words that are used in place of nouns.

Examples: he, she, it, they, him, them, her, him

Directions: Read each sentence. Write the pronoun that takes the place of each noun.

Example:

The **monkey** dropped the banana. ____It____

1. **Dad** washed the car last night. _____

2. **Noah** and **David** took a walk in the park. _____

3. **Peggy** spent the night at her grandmother's house. _____

4. The baseball **players** lost their game. _____

5. **Mike Van Meter** is a great soccer player. _____

6. The **parrot** can say five different words. _____

7. **Megan** wrote a story in class today. _____

8. They gave a party for **Teresa**. _____

9. Everyone in the class was happy for **Keiko**. _____

10. The children petted the **giraffe**. _____

11. Melita put the **kittens** near the warm stove. _____

Getting Possessive

Possessive pronouns show ownership.

Example: his hat, **her** shoes, **our** dog

We can use these pronouns before a noun:
my, **our**, **your**, **his**, **her**, **its**, **their**

Example: That is **my** bike.

We can use these pronouns on their own:
mine, **yours**, **ours**, **his**, **hers**, **theirs**, **its**

Example: That is **mine**.

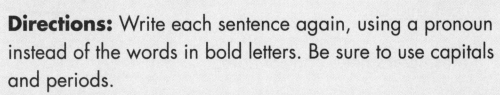

Directions: Write each sentence again, using a pronoun instead of the words in bold letters. Be sure to use capitals and periods.

Example:

My **dog's** bowl is brown.   **Its** bowl is brown.

1. That is **Lisa's** book.

   _____

2. This pencil is **my pencil**.

   _____

3. This hat is **your hat**.

   _____

4. Fifi is **Kevin's** cat.

   _____

5. That beautiful house is **our home**.

   _____

Wild for Pets

Adjectives are words that tell more about nouns, such as a **happy** child, a **cold** day or a **hard** problem. Adjectives can tell how many (**one** airplane) or which one (**those** shoes).

Directions: The nouns are in bold letters. Circle the adjectives that describe the nouns.

Example: Some people have (unusual) **pets**.

1. Some people keep wild **animals**, like lions and bears.

2. These **pets** need special care.

3. These **animals** want to be free when they get older.

4. Even small **animals** can be difficult if they are wild.

5. Raccoons and squirrels are not tame **pets**.

Directions: Complete the story below by writing in your own adjectives. Use your imagination.

My Cat

My cat is a very _____ animal. She has

_____ and _____ fur. Her favorite toy

is a _____ ball. She has _____ claws.

She has a _____ tail. She has a _____

face and _____ whiskers. I think she is the

_____ cat in the world!

Tell Me More!

Directions: Underline the nouns in each sentence below. Then, draw an arrow from each adjective to the noun it describes.

Example:

A <u>playpus</u> is a funny <u>animal</u> that lives in <u>Australia</u>.

1. This animal likes to swim.

2. The nose looks like a duck's bill.

3. It has a broad tail like a beaver.

4. Platypuses are great swimmers.

5. They have webbed feet which help them swim.

6. Their flat tails also help them move through the water.

7. The platypus is an unusual mammal because it lays eggs.

8. The eggs look like reptile eggs.

9. Platypuses can lay three eggs at a time.

Prefix Pros

Prefixes are special word parts added to the beginnings of words. Prefixes change the meaning of words.

Prefix	Meaning	Example
un	not	**un**happy
re	again	**re**do
pre	before	**pre**view
mis	wrong	**mis**understanding
dis	opposite	**dis**obey

Directions: Circle the word that begins with a prefix. Then, write the prefix and the root word.

1. The dog was unfriendly.

   _____ + _____

2. The movie preview was interesting.

   _____ + _____

3. The referee called an unfair penalty.

   _____ + _____

4. Please do not misbehave.

   _____ + _____

5. My parents disapprove of that show.

   _____ + _____

6. I had to redo the assignment.

   _____ + _____

Super Suffixes

Suffixes are word parts added to the ends of words.
Suffixes change the meaning of words.

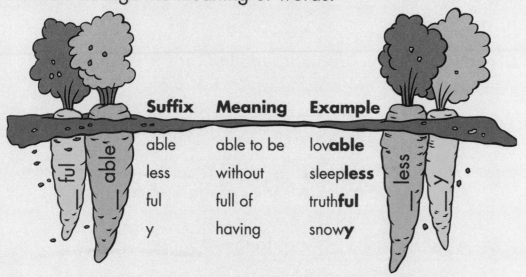

Suffix	Meaning	Example
able	able to be	lov**able**
less	without	sleep**less**
ful	full of	truth**ful**
y	having	snow**y**

Directions: Circle the suffix in each word below.

Example: fluff(y)

rainy	thoughtful	likeable
blameless	enjoyable	helpful
peaceful	careless	silky

Directions: Write a word for each meaning.

full of hope _____

having rain _____

without hope _____

able to break _____

without power _____

full of cheer _____

Web Weavers

A **verb** in a sentence is usually an action word, a word that tells what someone or something does. **Examples: run**, **jump**, **skip**.

Directions: Draw a box around the verb in each sentence below.

1. Spiders spin webs of silk.

2. A spider waits in the center of the web for its meals.

3. A spider sinks its sharp fangs into insects.

4. Spiders eat many insects.

5. Spiders make their nests with silk.

Directions: Choose the correct verb from the box and write it in the sentences below.

hides   swims   eat   grabs

1. A crab spider _____ deep inside a flower where it cannot be seen.

2. The crab spider _____ insects when they land on the flower.

3. The wolf spider is good because it

_____ wasps.

4. The water spider _____ under water.

Action All Around

When a verb tells what one person or thing is doing now, it usually ends in **s**. **Example:** She **sings**.

When a verb is used with **you**, **I** or **we**, we do not add an **s**.

Example: I **sing**.

Directions: Write the correct verb in each sentence.

I ___**write**___ a newspaper about our street.

writes   write

1. My sister _____ me sometimes.

   helps   help

2. She _____ the pictures.

   draw   draws

3. We _____ them together.

   delivers   deliver

4. I _____ the news about all the people.

   tell   tells

5. Mr. Macon _____ the most beautiful flowers.

   grow   grows

6. Mrs. Cohen _____ to her plants.

   talks   talk

7. Kevin Turner _____ his dog loose everyday.

   lets   let

9. You must _____ I live on an interesting street.

   thinks   think

Happy to Help

A **helping verb** is a verb that goes along with another verb.

Examples: might, **shall** and **are**

Directions: Write a helping verb from the box with each action verb.

can	could	must	might	may
would	should	will	shall	did
does	do	had	have	has
am	are	were	is	
be	being	been		

Example: Tomorrow, I _____ **might** _____ play soccer.

1. Mom _____ buy my new soccer shoes tonight.

2. Yesterday, my old soccer shoes _____ ripped by the cat.

3. I _____ going to ask my brother to go to the game.

4. He usually _____ not like soccer.

5. But, he _____ go with me because I am his sister.

6. He _____ promised to watch the entire soccer game.

7. He has _____ helping me with my homework.

8. I _____ spell a lot better because of his help.

It's All in the Past

The **past tense** of a verb tells about something that has already happened. We add a **d** or an **ed** to most verbs to show that something has already happened.

Directions: Use the verb from the first sentence to complete the second sentence.

Example:

Please **walk** the dog.

I already __walked__ her.

1. The flowers look good.

They _____ better yesterday.

2. Please accept my gift.

I _____ it for my sister.

3. I wonder who will win.

I _____ about it all night.

4. He will saw the wood.

He _____ some last week.

5. Fold the paper neatly.

She _____ her paper.

6. Let's cook outside tonight.

We _____ outside last night.

7. Do not block the way.

They _____ the entire street.

8. Follow my car.

We _____ them down the street.

No Time Like the Present

The **present tense** of a verb tells about something that is happening now, happens often or is about to happen. These verbs can be written two ways: The bird sing**s**. The bird is sing**ing**.

Directions: Write each sentence again, using the verb **is** and writing the **ing** form of the verb.

Example:

He cooks the cheeseburgers.

He is cooking the cheeseburgers.

1. Sharon dances to that song.

   _____

2. Frank washed the car.

   _____

3. Mr. Benson smiles at me.

   _____

Write a verb for the sentences below that tells something that is happening now. Be sure to use the verb **is** and the **ing** form of the verb.

Example:

The big, brown dog is barking_____.

1. The little baby _____.

2. Most nine-year-olds _____.

3. The monster on television _____.

Seeing the Future

The **future tense** of a verb tells about something that has not happened yet but will happen in the future. **Will** or **shall** is usually used with future tense.

Directions: Change the verb tense in each sentence to future tense.

Example:

She cooks dinner.

She will cook dinner.

1. He plays baseball.

_____

2. She walks to school.

_____

3. Samir talks to the teacher.

_____

4. I remember to vote.

_____

5. Jack mows the lawn every week.

_____

Out of the Ordinary

Irregular verbs are verbs that do not change from the present tense to the past tense in the regular way with **d** or **ed**.

Example: sing, **sang**

Directions: Read the sentence and underline the verbs. Choose the past-tense form from the box and write it next to the sentence.

blow — blew   fly — flew

come — came   give — gave

take — took   wear — wore

make — made   grow — grew

Example:

Dad will <u>make</u> a cake tonight.   <u>made</u>

1. I will probably grow another inch this year. _____

2. I will blow out the candles. _____

3. Everyone will give me presents. _____

4. I will wear my favorite red shirt. _____

5. My cousins will come from out of town. _____

6. It will take them four hours. _____

7. My Aunt Betty will fly in from Cleveland. _____

Breaking the Rules

Directions: Circle the verb that completes each sentence.

1. Scientists will try to (find, found) the cure.

2. Eric (brings, brought) his lunch to school yesterday.

3. Everyday, Betsy (sings, sang) all the way home.

4. Tomas (breaks, broke) the vase last night.

5. The ice had (freezes, frozen) in the tray.

6. Mitzi has (swims, swum) in that pool before.

7. Now I (choose, chose) to exercise daily.

8. The teacher has (rings, rung) the bell.

To Be or Not to Be

The verb **be** is different from all other verbs. The present-tense forms of **be** are **am**, **is** and **are**. The past-tense forms of **be** are **was** and **were**. The verb **to be** is written in the following ways:

singular: I am, you are, he is, she is, it is

plural: we are, you are, they are

Directions: Choose the correct form of be from the words in the box and write it in each sentence.

are	am	is	was	were

Example:

I _____ **am** _____ feeling good at this moment.

1. My sister _____ a good singer.

2. You _____ going to the store with me.

3. Emma _____ at the movies last week.

4. Marcos and Tom _____ best friends.

5. He _____ happy about the surprise.

6. The cat _____ hungry.

7. I _____ going to the ball game.

Think of a Link

Linking verbs connect the noun to a descriptive word. Linking verbs are often forms of the verb **be**.

Directions: The linking verb is underlined in each sentence. Circle the two words that are being connected.

Example: The (cat) is (fat.)

1. My favorite food is pizza.

2. The car was red.

3. I am tired.

4. Books are fun!

5. Pears taste juicy.

6. The airplane looks large.

Adverb Alert

Adverbs are words that usually describe verbs. They tell where, how or when.

Directions: Circle the adverb in each of the following sentences.

Example: The doctor worked (carefully.)

1. The skater moved gracefully across the ice.

2. Their call was returned quickly.

3. We easily learned the new words.

4. He did the work perfectly.

Directions: Complete the sentences below by writing your own adverbs in the blanks.

Example: The bees worked _____busily_____.

1. The dog barked _____.

2. The baby smiled _____.

3. She wrote her name _____.

Adverb Attitude

Directions: Read each sentence. Then, answer the questions on the lines below.

Example:

Charles ate hungrily.   **who?** __Charles__

what? _____ate_____   **how?** __hungrily__

1. She dances slowly.   **who?** _____

   what? _____   **how?** _____

2. The girl spoke carefully.   **who?** _____

   what? _____   **how?** _____

3. My brother ran quickly.   **who?** _____

   what? _____   **how?** _____

4. Olivia walks home often.   **who?** _____

   what? _____   **how?** _____

Preposition Prep

Prepositions show relationships between a noun or pronoun and another word in the sentence. The preposition comes before that noun or pronoun.

Example: The <u>book</u> is on the table.

Common Prepositions

above	behind	by	near	over
across	below	in	off	through
around	beside	inside	on	under

Directions: Circle the prepositions in each sentence.

1. The dog ran fast around the house.

2. The plates in the cupboard were clean.

3. Put the card inside the envelope.

4. The towel on the sink was wet.

5. I planted flowers in my garden.

6. My kite flew high above the trees.

7. The chair near the counter was sticky.

8. Under the ground, worms lived in their homes.

A Is for Article

Articles are words used before nouns. **A**, **an** and **the** are articles. We use **a** before words that begin with a consonant. We use **an** before words that begin with a vowel.

Example: a peach   **an apple**

Directions: Write **a** or **an** in the sentences below.

Example:

My bike had _____a_____ flat tire.

1. They brought _____ goat to the farm.

2. My mom wears _____ old pair of shoes to mow the lawn.

3. We had _____ party for my grandfather.

4. Everybody had _____ ice-cream cone after the game.

5. We bought _____ picnic table for our backyard.

6. We saw _____ lion sleeping in the shade.

7. It was _____ evening to be remembered.

8. He brought _____ blanket to the game.

9. _____ exit sign was above the door.

Comma Sense

Commas are used to separate words in a series of three or more.

Example:

My favorite fruits are apples, bananas and oranges.

Directions: Put commas where they are needed in each sentence.

1. Please buy milk eggs bread and cheese.

2. I need a folder paper and pencils for school.

3. Some good pets are cats dogs gerbils fish and rabbits.

4. Aaron Mike and Matt went to the baseball game.

5. Major forms of transportation are planes trains and automobiles.

Counting on Commas

We use commas to separate the day from the year.

Example: May 13, 1950

Directions: Write the dates in the blanks. Put the commas in and capitalize the name of each month.

Example:

Jack and Dave were born on february 22 1982.

February 22, 1982

1. My father's birthday is may 19 1948.

   _____

2. My sister was fourteen on december 13 1994.

   _____

3. Sonya's seventh birthday was on november 30 1998.

   _____

4. october 13 2009 was the last day I saw my lost cat.

   _____

5. On april 17 1997, we saw the Grand Canyon.

   _____

6. Our vacation lasted from april 2 2007
   to april 26 2007.

   _____

   _____

Let's Begin!

The names of **people**, **places** and **pets**, the **days of the week**, the **months of the year** and **holidays** begin with a capital letter.

Directions: Read the words in the box. Write the words in the correct column with capital letters at the beginning of each word.

ron polsky	tuesday	march
april	presidents' day	saturday
woofy	october	blackie
portland, oregon	corning, new york	molly yoder
valentine's day	fluffy	harold edwards
arbor day	bozeman, montana	sunday

People

_____

_____

_____

Places

_____

_____

_____

Pets

_____

_____

_____

Days

_____

_____

_____

Months

_____

_____

_____

Holidays

_____

_____

_____

Know Your Place

We capitalize the names of cities and states. We use a comma to separate the name of a city and a state.

Directions: Use capital letters and commas to write the names of the cities and states correctly.

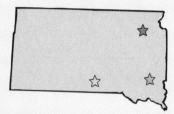

Example:

sioux falls south dakota

Sioux Falls, South Dakota

1. plymouth massachusettes

_____

2. boston massachusettes

_____

3. philadelphia pennsylvania

_____

4. white plains new york

_____

5. newport rhode island

_____

6. yorktown virginia

_____

Label It!

Nouns, pronouns, verbs, adjectives, adverbs and prepositions are all **parts of speech**.

Directions: Label the words in each sentence with the correct part of speech.

Example: The   cat   is   fat.

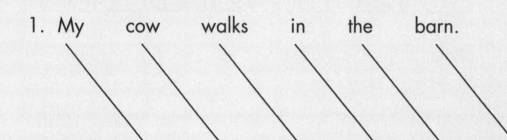

article   noun   verb   adjective

1. My   cow   walks   in   the   barn.

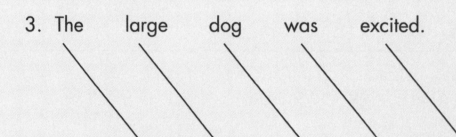

2. Red   flowers   grow   in   the   garden.

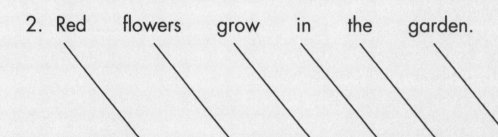

3. The   large   dog   was   excited.

Fill in a Story

Directions: Ask someone to give you nouns, verbs, adjectives and pronouns where shown. Write them in the blanks. Read the story to your friend when you finish.

The _____ Adventure
(adjective)

I went for a _____. I found a really
(noun)

big _____. It was so _____ that
(noun)   (adjective)

I _____ all the way home. I put it in
(verb)

my _____. To my amazement, it began
(noun)

to _____. I _____. I took it to
(verb)   (past-tense verb)

my _____. I showed it to all my _____.
(place)   (plural noun)

I decided to _____ it in a box and wrap it up
(verb)

with _____ paper. I gave it to _____
(adjective)   (person)

for a present. When _____ opened it, _____
(pronoun)   (pronoun)

_____. _____ shouted, "Thank you!
(past-tense verb)   (pronoun)

This is the best _____ I've ever had!"
(noun)

Zany Zebras

A **subject** tells who or what the sentence is about.

Directions: Underline the subject in the following sentences.

Example:

<u>The zebra</u> is a large animal.

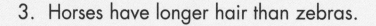

1. Zebras live in Africa.

2. Zebras are related to horses.

3. Horses have longer hair than zebras.

4. Zebras are good runners.

5. Their feet are protected by their hooves.

6. Some animals live in groups.

7. These groups are called herds.

8. Zebras live in herds with other grazing animals.

9. Grazing animals eat mostly grass.

Twice as Nice

Compound subjects are two or more nouns that have the same predicate.

Directions: Combine the subjects to create one sentence with a compound subject.

Example: Jill can swing.

Whitney can swing.

Luke can swing.

Jill, Whitney and Luke can swing.

1. Roses grow in the garden. Tulips grow in the garden.

   _____

   _____

2. Apples are fruit. Oranges are fruit. Bananas are fruit.

   _____

   _____

3. Bears live in the zoo. Monkeys live in the zoo.

   _____

   _____

4. Jackets keep us warm. Sweaters keep us warm.

   _____

   _____

Woodpecking Wonders

A **predicate** tells what the subject is doing, has done, or will do.

Directions: Underline the predicate in the following sentences.

Example: Woodpeckers <u>live in trees</u>.

1. They hunt for insects in the trees.

2. Woodpeckers have strong beaks.

3. They can peck through the bark.

4. The pecking sound can be heard from far away.

Directions: Circle the groups of words that can be predicates.

have long tongues	pick up insects
hole in bark	sticky substance
help it to climb trees	tree bark

Now, choose the correct predicates from above to finish these sentences.

1. Woodpeckers_____

   _____.

2. They use their tongues to_____

   _____.

3. Its strong feet _____

   _____.

Double the Action

Compound predicates have two or more verbs that have the same subject.

Directions: Combine the predicates to create one sentence with a compound predicate.

Example: We went to the zoo.
We watched the monkeys.
We went to the zoo and watched the monkeys.

1. Students read their books. Students do their work.

   _____

   _____

2. Dogs can bark loudly. Dogs can do tricks.

   _____

   _____

3. The football player caught the ball. The football player ran.

   _____

   _____

4. My dad sawed wood. My dad stacked wood.

   _____

   _____

5. My teddy bear sleeps with me. My teddy bear likes hugs.

   _____

   _____

Prickly Porcupines

Directions: Every sentence has two main parts—the subject and the predicate. Draw one line under the subject and two lines under the predicate in each sentence below.

Example:

Porcupines are related to mice and rats.

1. They are large rodents.

2. Porcupines have long, sharp quills.

3. The quills stand up straight when it is angry.

4. Most animals stay away from porcupines.

5. Their quills hurt other animals.

6. Porcupines sleep under rocks or bushes.

7. They sleep during the day.

8. Porcupines eat plants at night.

9. North America has some porcupines.

10. They are called New World porcupines.

11. New World porcupines can climb trees.

Putting It All Together

Directions: Draw one line under the subjects and two lines under the predicates in the sentences below.

1. My mom likes to plant flowers.

2. Our neighbors walk their dog.

3. Our car needs gas.

4. The children play house.

5. Movies and popcorn go well together.

6. Peanut butter and jelly is my favorite kind of sandwich.

7. Bill, Akiko and Brittany ride to the park.

8. We use pencils, markers and pens to write on paper.

9. Trees and shrubs need special care.

Shark Attack!

A **sentence** tells a complete idea.

Directions: Circle the groups of words that tell a complete idea.

1. Sharks are fierce hunters.

2. Afraid of sharks.

3. The great white shark will attack people.

4. Other kinds will not.

5. Sharks have an outer row of teeth for grabbing food.

6. When the outer teeth fall out, another row of teeth moves up.

7. Keep the ocean clean by eating dead animals.

8. Not a single bone in its body.

9. Cartilage.

10. Made of the same material as the tip of your nose.

11. Unlike other fish, sharks cannot float.

Downtown Discoveries

Directions: Complete the story, using sentences that tell complete ideas.

One morning, my friend asked me to take my first bus

trip downtown. I was so excited I _____

_____.

At the bus stop, we saw _____. Our bus driver

_____.

When we got off the bus _____

_____. I'd never seen so many

_____.

My favorite part was when we _____

_____.

We stopped to eat _____

_____

_____. I bought a _____

_____.

When we got home, I told my friend, " _____

_____

_____."

Wondering About Walruses

Statements are sentences that tell about something. Statements begin with a capital letter and end with a period. **Questions** are sentences that ask about something. Questions begin with a capital letter and end with a question mark.

Directions: Rewrite the sentences using capital letters and either a period or a question mark.

Example:

walruses live in the Arctic

Walruses live in the Arctic.

1. are walruses large sea mammals or fish

_____

2. they spend most of their time in the water and on ice

_____

3. are floating sheets of ice called ice floes

_____

4. are walruses related to seals

_____

5. their skin is thick, wrinkled and almost hairless

_____

Snow Day!

Exclamation points are used for sentences that express strong feelings. These sentences can have one or two words or be very long.

Example: Wait! or **Don't forget to call!**

Directions: Add an exclamation point at the end of sentences that express strong feelings. Add a period at the end of the statements.

1. My parents and I were watching television

2. The snow began falling around noon

3. Wow

4. The snow was really coming down

5. We turned the television off and looked out the window

6. The snow looked like a white blanket

7. How beautiful

8. We decided to put on our coats and go outside

9. Hurry

10. Get your sled

11. All the people on the street came out to see the snow

12. How wonderful

Contraction Action

Contractions are shortened forms of two words. We use apostrophes to show where letters are missing.

Example: It is = it's

Directions: Write the words that are used in each contraction.

we're _____ + _____   they'll _____ + _____

you'll _____ + _____   aren't _____ + _____

I'm _____ + _____   isn't _____ + _____

Directions: Write the contraction for the two words shown.

you have _____

have not _____

had not _____

we will _____

they are _____

he is _____

she had _____

it will _____

Make Your Mark

Apostrophes are used to show ownership by placing an **s** at the end of a single person, place or thing.

Example: Mary**'s** cat

Directions: Write the apostrophes in the contractions below.

Example: We shouldn**'**t be going to their house so late at night.

1. We didn t think that the ice cream would melt so fast.

2. They re never around when we re ready to go.

3. Didn t you need to make a phone call?

Directions: Add an apostrophe and an **s** to the words to show ownership of a person, place or thing.

Example: Jill**'s** bike is broken.

1. That is Holly   flower garden.

2. Ivan   new skates are black and green.

3. Mom threw away Dad   old shoes.

You Said It!

Quotation marks are punctuation marks that tell what is said by a person. Quotation marks go before the first word and after the punctuation of a direct quote. The first word of a direct quote begins with a capital letter.

Example: Katie said, "Never go in the water without a friend."

Directions: Put quotation marks around the correct words in the sentences below.

Example: "Wait for me, please," said Paloma.

1. John, would you like to visit a jungle? asked his uncle.

2. The police officer said, Don't worry, we'll help you.

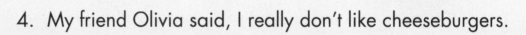

3. James shouted, Hit a home run!

4. My friend Olivia said, I really don't like cheeseburgers.

Directions: Write your own quotations by answering the questions below. Be sure to put quotation marks around your words.

1. What would you say if you saw a dinosaur?

_____

_____

2. What would your best friend say if your hair turned purple?

_____

_____

Taking a Ride

Directions: Put quotation marks around the correct words in the sentences below.

1. Can we go for a bike ride? asked Katrina.

   _____

   _____

2. Yes, said Mom.

   _____

3. Let's go to the park, said Mike.

   _____

4. Great idea! said Mom.

   _____

5. How long until we get there? asked Katrina.

   _____

   _____

6. Soon, said Mike.

   _____

7. Here we are! exclaimed Mom.

   _____

What's It All About?

A **topic sentence** is usually the first sentence in a paragraph. It tells what the story will be about.

Directions: Read the following sentences. Circle the topic sentence that should go first in the paragraph that follows.

Rainbows have seven colors.

There's a pot of gold.

I like rainbows.

The colors are red, orange, yellow, green, blue, indigo and violet. Red forms the outer edge, with violet on the inside of the rainbow.

He cut down a cherry tree.

His wife was named Martha.

George Washington was a good president.

He helped our country get started. He chose intelligent leaders to help him run the country.

Mark Twain was a great author.

Mark Twain was unhappy sometimes.

Mark Twain was born in Missouri.

One of his most famous books is *Huckleberry Finn*. He wrote many other great books.

Middle Matters

Middle sentences support the topic sentence. They tell more about it.

Directions: Underline the middle sentences that support each topic sentence below.

Topic Sentence:

Penguins are birds that cannot fly.

Pelicans can spear fish with their sharp bills.

Many penguins waddle or hop about on land.

Even though they cannot fly, they are excellent swimmers.

Pelicans keep their food in a pouch.

Topic Sentence:

Volleyball is a team sport in which the players hit the ball over the net.

There are two teams with six players on each team.

My friend John would rather play tennis with Akiko.

Players can use their heads or their hands.

I broke my hand once playing handball.

Topic Sentence:

Pikes Peak is the most famous of all the Rocky Mountains.

Some mountains have more trees than other mountains.

Many people like to climb to the top.

Many people like to ski and camp there, too.

The weather is colder at the top of most mountains.

Wrapping It Up

Ending sentences are sentences that tie the story together.

Directions: Choose the correct ending sentence for each story from the sentences below. Write it at the end of the paragraph.

It was a new pair of shoes!

It was all the corn on the cob I could eat!

It was a new eraser!

Corn on the Cob

Corn on the cob used to be my favorite food. That is, until I lost my four front teeth. For one whole year, I had to sit and watch everyone else eat my favorite food without me. Mom gave me creamed corn, but it just wasn't the same. When my teeth finally came in, Dad said he had a surprise for me. I thought I was going to get a bike or a new C.D. player or something. I was just as happy to get what I did.

_____

I would like to take a train ride every year.

Trains move faster than I thought they would.

She had brought her new gerbil along for the ride.

A Train Ride

When our family took its first train ride, my sister brought along a big box. She would not tell anyone what she had in it. In the middle of the trip, we heard a sound coming from the box. "Okay, Kate, now you have to open the box," said Mom. When she opened the box we were surprised.

_____

Spelling

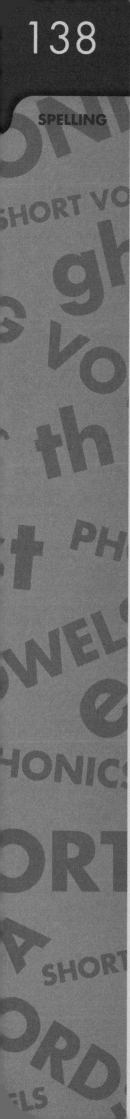

Which Is Witch?

Homophones are words that sound the same but are spelled differently and have different meanings.

Directions: Use the homophones in the box to answer the riddles below.

main	peace	dear	to
mane	piece	deer	too

1. Which word has the word **pie** in it? Piece

2. Which word rhymes with **ear** and is an animal? dear

3. Which word rhymes with **shoe** and means **also**? too

4. Which word has the same letters as the word **read** but in a different order? main

5. Which word rhymes with **train** and is something on a pony? _____

6. Which word, if it began with a capital letter, might be the name of an important street? _____

7. Which word sounds like a number but has only two letters? _____

8. Which word rhymes with the last syllable in **police** and can mean quiet? _____

The Same but Different

Directions: Write a word from the box to complete each sentence.

main	meat	dear	two
mane	meet	deer	too

1. The horse had a long, beautiful _____.

   The _____ idea of the paragraph was boats.

2. Let's _____ at my house to do our homework.

   The lion was fed _____ at mealtime.

3. We had _____ kittens.

   Jaden has a red bike. Tom does, _____.

4. The _____ ran in front of the car.

   I begin my letters with " _____Mom."

Let's Hear It for Homophones!

Directions: Circle the word in each sentence which is not spelled correctly. Then, write the word correctly.

1. Please meat me at the park.

   _____

2. I would like a peace of pie.

   _____

3. There were too cookies left.

   _____

4. The horse's main needed to be brushed.

   _____

5. We saw a dear in the forest.

   _____

Busy Bees

Directions: Cut out each honeybee at the bottom of the page and glue it on the flower with its homophone.

cut ✂ -

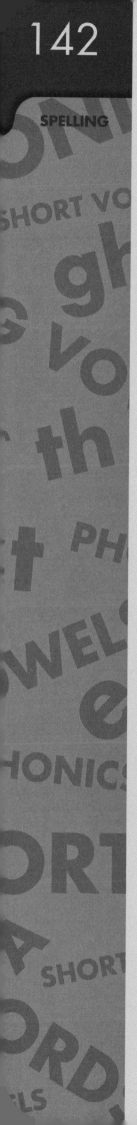

This page is blank for the cutting activity
on the opposite side.

Time to Rhyme!

Directions: Use homophones to create two-lined rhymes.

Example: I found it a **pain**

To comb the horse's **mane**!

1. _____

_____

2. _____

_____

3. _____

_____

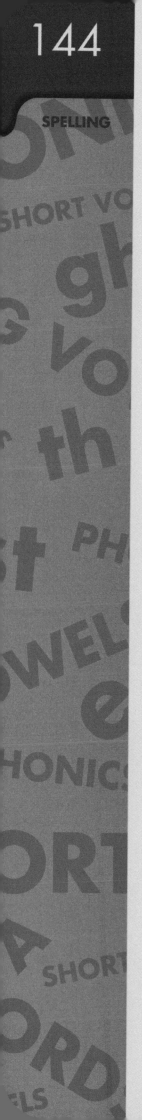

Clue Me In!

Short vowel patterns usually have a single vowel followed by a consonant sound.

Short a is the sound you hear in the word **can**.
Short e is the sound you hear in the word **men**.
Short i is the sound you hear in the word **pig**.
Short o is the sound you hear in the word **pot**.
Short u is the sound you hear in the word **truck**.

fast   track   spin   lunch   bread   block

Directions: Use the words in the box to answer the questions below.

Which word:

begins with the same sound
as **blast** and ends with the
same sound as **look**?   _____

rhymes with **stack**?   _____

begins with the same sound as
phone and ends with the
same sound as **lost**?   _____

has the same vowel sound
as **hen**?   _____

rhymes with **crunch**?   _____

begins with the same sound as
spot and ends with the same
sound as **can**?   _____

Picture This!

Directions: Use the words in the box to complete each sentence.

fast	wish	truck	bread	sun
best	stop	track	lunch	block

Race cars can go very _____.

Ana packs a _____ for Carlos before school.

Throw a penny in the well and make

a _____.

The _____ had a flat tire.

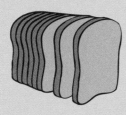

My favorite kind of _____ is whole wheat.

Find It, Fix It

Directions: Circle the word in each sentence which is not spelled correctly. Then, write the word correctly.

1. Be sure to stopp at the red light.

_____

2. The train goes down the trak.

_____

3. Please put the bred in the toaster.

_____

4. I need another blok to finish.

_____

5. The beasst player won a trophy.

_____

6. Blow out the candles and make a wiish.

_____

Say It Long

Long vowels are the letters **a, e, i, o** and **u** which say the letter name sound.

Long a is the sound you hear in **cane**.
Long e is the sound you hear in **green**.
Long i is the sound you hear in **pie**.
Long o is the sound you hear in **bowl**.
Long u is the sound you hear in **cube**.

| lame | goal | pain | few | street |
| fright | nose | gray | bike | fuse |

Directions: Use the words in the box to answer the questions below.

1   Add one letter to each of these words to make words from the box.

   ray _____   use _____

   right _____

2. Change one letter from each word to make a word from the box.

   pail _____   goat _____

   late _____   bite _____

3. Write the word from the box that . . .

   has the long **e** sound.   _____

   rhymes with **you**.   _____

   is a homophone for **knows**.   _____

Getting A-Long with Vowels

Directions: Use the words in the box to complete each sentence.

goal	pain	few	bike
street	fright	nose	gray

1. Look both ways before crossing

   the _____.

2. My _____ had a flat tire.

3. Our walk through the haunted house

   gave us such a _____.

4. I kicked the soccer ball and scored a _____.

5. The _____ clouds mean
   rain is coming.

6. Cover your _____ when you sneeze.

Use the Clues!

Directions: Use long vowel words from the box to answer the clues below. Write the letters of the words on the lines.

few	bike	dime	goal	fuse
lame	street	nose	fright	pain

1. __ __ __ __ __ [□]   (rhymes with **night**)

2. __ __ [□] __ __ __   (could be Main or Maple)

3. __ [□] __   (synonym for **a couple**)

4. __ __ [□] __   (rhymes with **tame**)

5. __ __ __ [□]   (can be ridden on a trail)

6. __ __ __ [□]   (homophone for **pane**)

7. [□] __ __ __   (ten of these make a dollar)

8. __ [□] __ __   (changing one letter of this word makes **goat**)

9. __ [□] __ __   (has the word **use** in it)

10. __ __ [□] __   (homophone for **knows**)

Now, read the letters in the boxes from top to bottom to find out what kind of a job you did!

Pick a Word

The **k** sound can be spelled with a **c**, **k** or **ck** after a short vowel sound.

Directions: Use the words from the box to complete the sentences. Use each word only once.

crowd	keeper
cost	pack
kangaroo	thick

1. On sunny days, there is always a _____ of people at the zoo.

2. It doesn't _____ much to get into the zoo.

3. We always get hungry, so we _____ a picnic lunch.

4. We like to watch the _____.

5. Its _____ tail helps it jump and walk.

6. The _____ always makes sure the cages are clean.

The Zoo's Kangaroos

Directions: Use **c**, **k**, or **ck** words to complete this story. Some of the verbs are past tense and need to end with **ed**.

One day, Kevin and I _____ a lunch

and went to the zoo. There was a big _____

of people. Kevin wanted to see the _____ .

When we got to the _____ cage, we

met the _____ , whose name was Carla.

"How much does it _____ $ to keep a

_____ ?" Kevin asked

the _____ . "Our grass at home is really

_____ NOT THIN , and that's what

_____ eat, right?"

"You must have a big cage and clean it every day,"

Carla the _____ told Kevin. Kevin got

quiet very quickly. "I'll just keep coming here to see

_____ in the cage you clean," he said.

The Super Sounds of S

The **s** sound can be spelled with an **s**, **ss**, **c** or **ce**.

Directions: Use the words from the box to complete the sentences below. Write each word only once.

center	pencil	space
address	police	darkness

1. I drew a circle in the _____ of the page.

2. I'll write to you if you tell me your _____.

3. She pushed too hard and broke the point on

   her _____.

4. If you hear a noise at night, call the _____.

5. It was night, and I couldn't see him in

   the _____.

6. There's not enough _____ for me to sit
   next to you.

Sssspelling!

Directions: Write the words from the box that answer the questions.

center   pencil   space   address   police   darkness

1. Which words spell the **s** sound with **ss**?

   _____

2. Which words spell **s** with a **c**?

   _____

3. Which words spell **s** with **ce**?

   _____

4. Write two other words you know that spell **s** with an **s**.

   _____

5. Put these letters in order to make words from the box.

   sdsdera   _____

   sdserakn   _____

   clipoe   _____

   clipne   _____

   capse   _____

   retnce   _____

Off to a Good Start

Directions: Match each sentence with the word which completes it. Then, write the word on the line.

1. The farmer was _____ •   • input
   because it didn't rain.

2. The scientist tried to   •   • unhappy

   _____ secret formula.

3. The child _____ his   •   • disagree
   report into the computer.

4. We were _____ to   •   • replay
   do the work without help.

5. My brother and I _____   •   • discover
   about which show to watch.

6. The umpire called for a   •   • inside

   _____ of the game.

7. We had to stay _____   •   • unable
   when it got cold.

That's the End!

A **suffix** is a word part added to the end of a word. Suffixes add to or change the meaning of the word.

Example: sad + ly = sadly

Below are some suffixes and their meanings.

ment	state of being, quality of, act of
ly	like or in a certain way
ness	state of being
ful	full of
less	without

Directions: The words in the box have suffixes. Use the suffix meanings above to match each word with its meaning below. Write the words on the lines.

> friendly   cheerful   safely   sleeveless speechless
>
> kindness   amazement   sickness   peaceful   excitement

1. in a safe way   __ __ __ __ __ __
                                    6

2. full of cheer   __ __ __ __ __ __ __
                                          2

3. full of peace   __ __ __ __ __ __ __ __
                              4

4. state of   __ __ __ __ __ __ __ __ __
   being amazed   5

5. state of   __ __ __ __ __ __ __ __ __
   being excited   1

6. without speech __ __ __ __ __ __ __ __ __ __ __
                                          3

Use the numbered letters to find the missing word below. You are now on your way to becoming a

__ __ __ __ __ __ of suffixes!
5   6   3   1   4   2

Short and Sweet

A **contraction** is a short way to write two words together. Some letters are left out, but an apostrophe takes their place.

Directions: Write the words from the box that answer the questions.

| hasn't | you've | aren't | we've | weren't |

1. Write the correct contractions below.

Example:

I have   _____I've_____

was not   _____wasn't_____

we have   _____

you have   _____

are not   _____

were not   _____

has not   _____

2. Write two words from the box that are contractions using **have**.

_____   _____

3. Write three words from the box that are contractions using **not**.

_____   _____

_____

Math

Mad to Add

Directions: Add.

Example:

Add the ones.   Add the tens.

$$
\begin{array}{r} 26 \\ +21 \\ \hline 7 \end{array}
\qquad
\begin{array}{r} 26 \\ +21 \\ \hline 47 \end{array}
$$

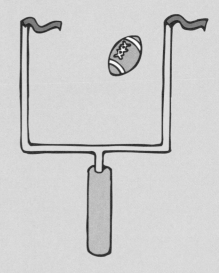

$$
\begin{array}{r} 18 \\ +11 \\ \hline \end{array}
\quad
\begin{array}{r} 24 \\ +35 \\ \hline \end{array}
\quad
\begin{array}{r} 38 \\ +21 \\ \hline \end{array}
\quad
\begin{array}{r} 49 \\ +50 \\ \hline \end{array}
\quad
\begin{array}{r} 52 \\ +33 \\ \hline \end{array}
$$

$$
\begin{array}{r} 75 \\ +12 \\ \hline \end{array}
\quad
\begin{array}{r} 83 \\ +16 \\ \hline \end{array}
\quad
\begin{array}{r} 67 \\ +32 \\ \hline \end{array}
\quad
\begin{array}{r} 44 \\ +25 \\ \hline \end{array}
\quad
\begin{array}{r} 28 \\ +41 \\ \hline \end{array}
$$

68 + 20 = _____   54 + 25 = _____   71 + 17 = _____

The Lions scored 42 points. The Clippers scored 21 points. How many points were scored in all?

_____

Sum It Up

Directions: Study the example. Add using regrouping.

Example:

```
  5,356
+ 3,976
-------
  9,332
```

Steps:

1. Add the ones.

2. Regroup the tens.
   Add the tens.

3. Regroup the hundreds.
   Add the hundreds.

4. Add the thousands.

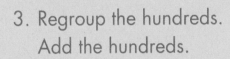

```
  6,849          1,846          9,221
+ 3,276        + 8,384        + 6,769
```

```
  2,758          5,299          7,932
+ 3,663        + 8,764        + 6,879
```

A plane flew 1,838 miles on the first day. It flew 2,347 miles on the second day. How many miles did it fly in all?

_____

Mental Math: Add On!

Directions: Try to do these addition problems in your head without using paper and pencil.

7	6	8	10	2
+4	+3	+1	+ 2	+9

10	40	80	60	50
+20	+20	+100	+30	+70

350	300	400	450	680
+150	+500	+800	+ 10	+100

	4,000	300	8,000	
1,000	400	200	500	9,800
+ 200	+ 30	+ 80	+ 60	+ 150

01-335141120

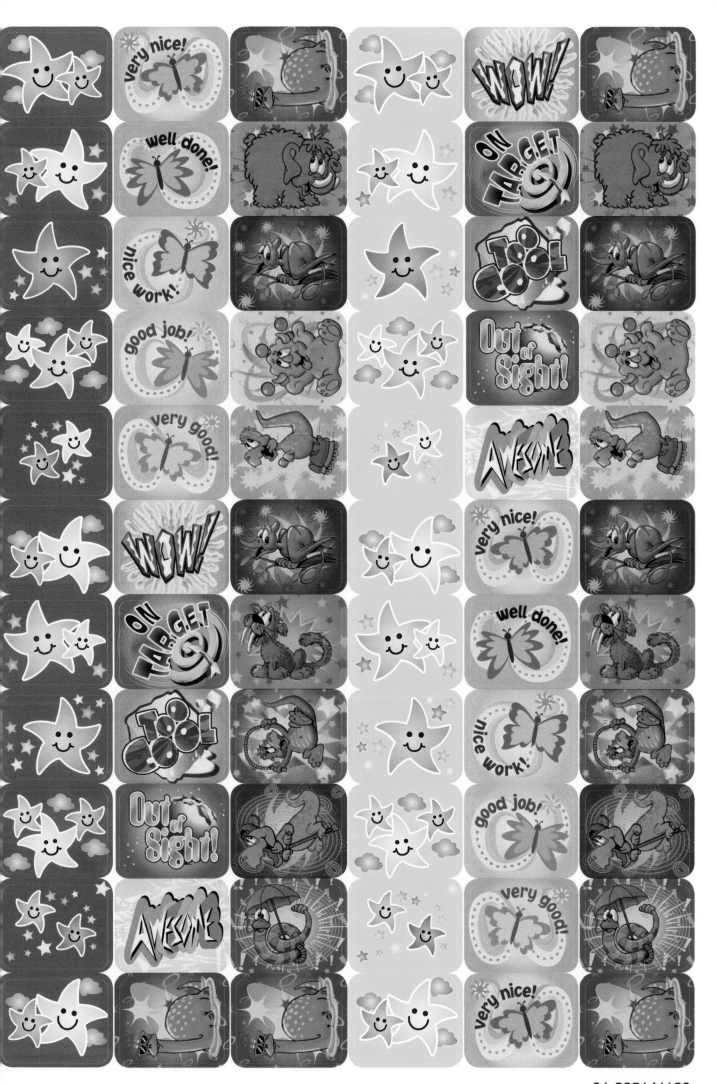

What's the Difference?

Subtraction means "taking away" or subtracting one number from another to find the difference. For example, 10 - 3 = 7.

Directions: Subtract.

Example: Subtract the ones.   Subtract the tens.

$$\begin{array}{r} 39 \\ -24 \\ \hline 5 \end{array} \qquad \begin{array}{r} 39 \\ -24 \\ \hline 15 \end{array}$$

$$\begin{array}{r} 48 \\ -35 \\ \hline \end{array} \qquad \begin{array}{r} 95 \\ -22 \\ \hline \end{array} \qquad \begin{array}{r} 87 \\ -16 \\ \hline \end{array} \qquad \begin{array}{r} 55 \\ -43 \\ \hline \end{array}$$

$$\begin{array}{r} 37 \\ -14 \\ \hline \end{array} \qquad \begin{array}{r} 69 \\ -57 \\ \hline \end{array} \qquad \begin{array}{r} 44 \\ -23 \\ \hline \end{array} \qquad \begin{array}{r} 99 \\ -78 \\ \hline \end{array}$$

66 – 44 = _____   57 – 33 = _____

The yellow car traveled 87 miles per hour. The orange car traveled 66 miles per hour. How much faster was the yellow car traveling?

_____

Ready to Regroup

Directions: Study the example. Add using regrouping.

Example:

```
  634
 -455
  179
```

Steps:

1. Subtract ones. You cannot subtract five ones from 4 ones.

2. Regroup ones by regrouping 3 tens to 2 tens + 10 ones.

3. Subtract 5 ones from 14 ones.

4. Regroup tens by regrouping hundreds (5 hundreds + 10 tens).

5. Subtract 5 tens from 12 tens.

6. Subtract hundreds.

635	553	832	944	423
−169	−174	−563	−578	−268

941	733	266	387	594
−872	−498	−197	−198	−385

Bailey goes to school 185 days a year.
Yoko goes to school 313 days a year.
How many more days of school does Yoko
attend each year?

_____

Mental Math: Take It Away!

Directions: Try to do these subtraction problems in your head without using paper and pencil.

9	12	7	5	15
−3	− 6	−6	−1	− 5

40	90	100	20	60
−20	−80	− 50	−20	−10

450	500	250	690	320
−250	−300	− 20	−100	− 20

1,000	8,000	7,000	4,000	9,500
− 400	− 500	− 900	−2,000	−4,000

Round and Round We Go

If the ones number is 5 or greater, "round up" to the nearest 10. If the ones number is 4 or less, the tens number stays the same and the ones number becomes a zero.

Examples:

1<u>5</u> round <u>up</u> to 20

2<u>3</u> round <u>down</u> to 20

4<u>7</u> round <u>up</u> to 50

7 _____   58 _____

12 _____   81 _____

33 _____   94 _____

27 _____   44 _____

73 _____   88 _____

25 _____   66 _____

39 _____   70 _____

Round to the Right

If the tens number is 5 or greater, "round up" to the nearest hundred. If the tens number is 4 or less, the hundreds number remains the same.

REMEMBER. . . Look at the number directly to the right of the place to which you are rounding.

Examples:

2<u>3</u>0 round <u>down</u> to 200

1<u>5</u>0 round <u>up</u> to 200

4<u>7</u>0 round <u>up</u> to 500

7<u>3</u>2 round <u>down</u> to 700

456 _____   120 _____

340 _____   923 _____

867 _____   550 _____

686 _____   231 _____

770 _____   492 _____

Oh, My, Let's Multiply!

Multiplication is a short way to find the sum of adding the same number a certain amount of times. For example, we write $7 \times 4 = 28$ instead of $7 + 7 + 7 + 7 = 28$.

Directions: Study the example. Multiply.

Example:

There are two groups of seashells.
There are 3 seashells in each group. $2 \times 3 = 6$
How many seashells are there in all?

$4 + 4 =$ ____ $3 + 3 + 3 =$ ____

$2 \times 4 =$ ____ $3 \times 3 =$ ____

2	3	4	6	7
x3	x5	x3	x2	x3

5	6	4	7	8
x2	x3	x2	x2	x3

5	9	8	6	9
x5	x4	x5	x6	x3

Something's Fishy!

Factors are the numbers multiplied together in a multiplication problem. The answer is called the *product*. If you change the order of the factors, the product stays the same.

Example:

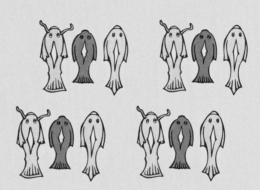

There are 4 groups of fish.
There are 3 fish in each group.
How many fish are there in all?

$$4 \times 3 = 12$$
factor x factor = product

Directions: Draw 3 groups of 4 fish.

$$3 \times 4 = 12$$

Compare your drawing and answer with the example. What did you notice?

Directions: Fill in the missing numbers. Multiply.

5 x 4 = _____	3 x 6 = _____	4 x 2 = _____
4 x 5 = _____	6 x 3 = _____	2 x 4 = _____

3	7	2	9	8	4
x7	x3	x9	x2	x4	x8

5	2	6	3	5	6
x2	x5	x3	x6	x6	x5

Good Times!

Directions: Time yourself as you multiply. How quickly can you complete this page?

3	8	1	1	3
x2	x7	x0	x6	x4

4	4	2	9	9
x1	x4	x5	x3	x9

0	2	9	8	7
x8	x6	x6	x5	x3

3	2	4	1	0
x5	x0	x6	x3	x0

Factor Facts

Directions: Complete the multiplication table. Use it to practice your multiplication facts.

X	0	1	2	3	4	5	6	7	8	9	10
0	0										
1		1									
2			4								
3				9							
4					16						
5						25					
6							36				
7								49			
8									64		
9										81	
10											100

Dare to Divide

Division is a way to find out how many times one number is contained in another number. For example, 28 ÷ 4 = 7 means that there are seven groups of four in 28.

Directions: Study the example. Divide.

Example:

There are 6 oars.
Each canoe needs 2 oars.
How many canoes can be used?

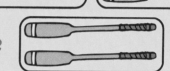

Circle groups of 2.
There are 3 groups of 2.

6	÷	2	=	3
oars		number of oars needed per canoe		canoes

9 ÷ 3 = _____   8 ÷ 2 = _____   16 ÷ 4 = _____

15 ÷ 5 = _____   18 ÷ 2 = _____   20 ÷ 4 = _____

21 ÷ 7 = _____   24 ÷ 6 = _____   12 ÷ 2 = _____

Sail Away!

Directions: Divide. Draw a line from the boat to the sail with the correct answer.

Dive in to Division

Division is a way to find out how many times one number is contained in another number. The ÷ sign means "divided by." Another way to divide is to use ⌐. The dividend is the larger number that is divided by the smaller number, or divisor. The answer of a division problem is called the *quotient*.

Directions: Study the example. Divide.

Example:

$$20 \div 4 = 5$$

dividend   divisor   quotient

$$\overset{\text{quotient}}{\underset{\text{divisor} \quad \text{dividend}}{4 \overline{)\,20\,}^{5}}}$$

$35 \div 7 =$ ___ $7\overline{)\,35\,}$ $42 \div 6 =$ ___ $6\overline{)\,42\,}$

$2\overline{)\,12\,}$ $3\overline{)\,18\,}$ $4\overline{)\,36\,}$ $5\overline{)\,50\,}$

$6\overline{)\,24\,}$ $7\overline{)\,21\,}$ $8\overline{)\,32\,}$ $9\overline{)\,27\,}$

$36 \div 6 =$ _____ $28 \div 4 =$ _____

$15 \div 5 =$ _____ $12 \div 2 =$ _____

A tree farm has 36 trees. There are 4 rows of trees. How many trees are there in each row?

_____

What's Left?

Division is a way to find out how many times one number is contained in another number. For example, $28 \div 4 = 7$ means that there are seven groups of four in 28. The dividend is the larger number that is divided by the smaller number, or divisor. The quotient is the answer in a division problem. The remainder is the amount left over. The remainder is always less than the divisor.

Directions: Study the example. Find each quotient and remainder.

Example:

There are 11 dog biscuits. Put them in groups of 3. There are 2 left over.

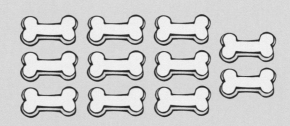

$$3 \overline{\smash{\big)}\ 11}^{\ \ 3} \qquad 3 \overline{\smash{\big)}\ 11}^{\ \ 3\ r2}$$
$$\underline{-9}$$
$$2 \text{ remainder}$$

Remember: The remainder must be less than the **divisor**!

$$3 \overline{\smash{\big)}\ 13} \qquad 4 \overline{\smash{\big)}\ 17} \qquad 6 \overline{\smash{\big)}\ 32} \qquad 5 \overline{\smash{\big)}\ 26}$$

$$9 \div 4 = \underline{\qquad} \qquad\qquad 12 \div 5 = \underline{\qquad}$$

$$26 \div 4 = \underline{\qquad} \qquad\qquad 49 \div 9 = \underline{\qquad}$$

The pet store has 7 cats. Two cats go in each cage. How many cats are left over?

$$\underline{\qquad}$$

Rules to Remember

A number is divisible...

by 2 if the last digit is 0 or even (2, 4, 6, 8).
by 3 if the sum of all digits is divisible by 3.
by 4 if the last two digits are divisible by 4.
by 5 if the last digit is a 0 or 5.
by 10 if the last digit is 0.

Example: 250 is divisible by 2, 5, 10

Directions: Tell what numbers each of these numbers is divisible by.

3,732 _____   439 _____

50 _____   444 _____

7,960 _____   8,212 _____

104,924 _____   2,345 _____

Factor Trees

Factors are the smaller numbers multiplied together to make a larger number. Factor trees are one way to find all the factors of a number.

Example:

24
6 x 4
2 x 3 x 2 x 2

40
8 x ___
4 x ___ x ___
___ x ___ x ___ x ___

36
6 x ___
3 x ___ x ___ x ___

81
___ x ___
___ x ___ x ___ x ___

12
___ x 4
___ x ___ x ___

Following Orders

When you solve a problem that involves more than one operation, this is the order to follow:

      ( ) Parentheses first

      x Multiplication

      ÷ Division

      + Addition

      – Subtraction

Example:

$$2 + (3 \times 5) - 2 = 15$$
$$2 + 15 - 2 = 15$$
$$17 - 2 = 15$$

Directions: Solve the problems using the correct order of operations.

$(5 - 3) + 4 \times 7 =$ _____ $1 + 2 \times 3 + 4 =$ _____

$6 \times 3 - 1 =$ _____ $(8 \div 2) \times 4 =$ _____

$9 \div 3 \times 3 + 0 =$ _____ $5 - 2 \times 1 + 2 =$ _____

Let's Operate!

Directions: Use +, −, x and ÷ to complete the problems so the number sentence is true.

Example: 4 __+__ 2 __−__ 1 = 5

(8 ___ 2) ___ 4 = 8

(1 ___ 2) ___ 3 = 1

9 ___ 3 ___ 9 = 3

(7 ___ 5) ___ 1 = 2

8 ___ 5 ___ 4 = 10

5 ___ 4 ___ 1 = 1

Perfect Percentages

A percentage is the amount of a number out of 100. This is the percent sign: %

Directions: Fill in the blanks.

Example: $70\% = \dfrac{\mathbf{70}}{100}$ $\mathbf{40}\% = \dfrac{40}{100}$

$30\% = \dfrac{}{100}$ $\qquad\qquad$ $10\% = \dfrac{}{100}$

$90\% = \dfrac{}{100}$ $\qquad\qquad$ $40\% = \dfrac{}{100}$

$70\% = \dfrac{}{100}$ $\qquad\qquad$ $80\% = \dfrac{}{100}$

$\underline{}\% = \dfrac{20}{100}$ $\qquad\qquad$ $\underline{}\% = \dfrac{60}{100}$

$\underline{}\% = \dfrac{30}{100}$ $\qquad\qquad$ $\underline{}\% = \dfrac{10}{100}$

$\underline{}\% = \dfrac{50}{100}$ $\qquad\qquad$ $\underline{}\% = \dfrac{90}{100}$

Pick the Parts

A fraction is a number that names part of a whole, such as $\frac{1}{2}$ or $\frac{1}{3}$.

Directions: Write the fraction that tells what part of each figure is colored. The first one is done for you.

Example:

2 parts shaded
5 parts in the whole figure

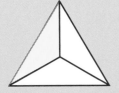

$\frac{1}{3}$

_____   _____   _____

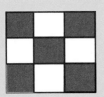

_____   _____   _____

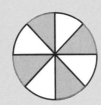

_____   _____   _____

It's All the Same to Me

Fractions that name the same part of a whole are equivalent fractions.

Example: $\dfrac{1}{2} = \dfrac{2}{4}$

Directions: Fill in the numbers to complete the equivalent fractions.

$\dfrac{1}{4} = \dfrac{\square}{8}$

$\dfrac{2}{3} = \dfrac{\square}{6}$

$\dfrac{1}{6} = \dfrac{\square}{12}$

$\dfrac{2}{3} = \dfrac{\square}{6}$

$\dfrac{1}{3} = \dfrac{\square}{12}$ $\dfrac{1}{5} = \dfrac{\square}{15}$

$\dfrac{1}{4} = \dfrac{\square}{8}$ $\dfrac{1}{2} = \dfrac{\square}{6}$

$\dfrac{2}{3} = \dfrac{\square}{9}$ $\dfrac{2}{6} = \dfrac{\square}{18}$

Care to Compare?

Directions: Circle the fraction in each pair that is larger.

Example:

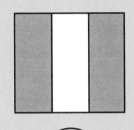   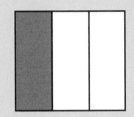

$\left(\dfrac{2}{3}\right)$ $\dfrac{1}{3}$

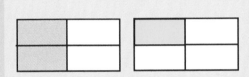

$\dfrac{2}{4}$ $\dfrac{1}{4}$ $\dfrac{1}{8}$ $\dfrac{2}{8}$

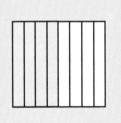   

$\dfrac{1}{2}$ $\dfrac{1}{3}$ $\dfrac{2}{3}$ $\dfrac{1}{6}$

$\dfrac{1}{4}$ or $\dfrac{1}{6}$ $\dfrac{1}{5}$ or $\dfrac{1}{7}$ $\dfrac{1}{8}$ or $\dfrac{1}{4}$

Get to the Point

A decimal is a number with one or more numbers to the right of a decimal point. A decimal point is a dot placed between the ones place and the tens place of a number, such as 2.5.

Example:

$\frac{3}{10}$ can be written as .3 They are both read as three-tenths.

Directions: Write the answer as a decimal for the shaded parts.

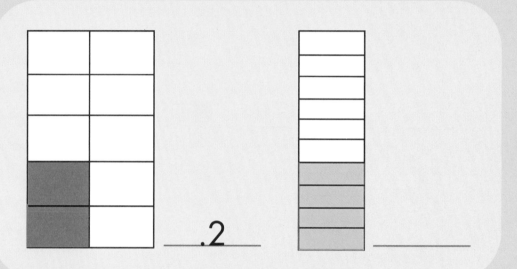

___.2___   _____

Directions: Color parts of each object to match the decimals given.

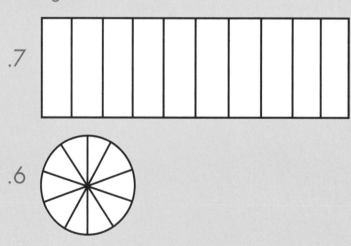

.7

.6

.5

Make a Match

A decimal is a number with one or more numbers to the right of a decimal point, such as 6.5 or 2.25. Equivalent means numbers that are equal.

Directions: Draw a line between the equivalent numbers.

.8 $\frac{5}{10}$

five-tenths $\frac{8}{10}$

.7 $\frac{6}{10}$

.4   .3

six-tenths $\frac{2}{10}$

three-tenths $\frac{7}{10}$

.2 $\frac{9}{10}$

nine-tenths $\frac{4}{10}$

Decimal Dash

Decimals are added and subtracted in the same way as other numbers. Simply carry down the decimal point to your answer.

Directions: Add or subtract.

Examples:

```
   1
   1.3              4.5
 +2.8            −2.2
 ─────           ─────
   4.1              2.3
```

```
   1.3      4.6      5.1      6.7
 +2.2     −3.4     +8.8     −4.3
 ─────    ─────    ─────    ─────
```

```
   7.9      6.4     11.4      0.5
 −3.7     −3.7     −3.7     −3.7
 ─────    ─────    ─────    ─────
```

9.3 + 1.2 = _____

2.5 − 0.7 = _____

1.2 + 5.0 = _____

Bob jogs around the school every day. The distance for one time around is .7 of a mile. If he jogs around the school two times, how many miles does he jog each day?

_____

Pattern Play

Directions: Follow the pattern: ●■▲☆ to get through the maze.

START

FINISH

Crack the Color Code!

Geometry is the branch of mathematics that has to do with points, lines and shapes.

 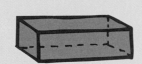

cube   rectangular prism   cone   cylinder   sphere

Directions: Use the code to color the picture.

Color:

cubes = **blue**

rectangular prisms = **red**

cones = **green**

cylinders = yellow

spheres = **orange**

Get in Line!

Geometry is the branch of mathematics that has to do with points, lines and shapes.

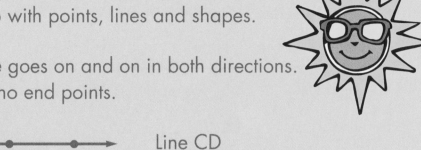

A **line** goes on and on in both directions. It has no end points.

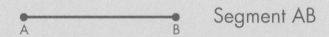 Line CD

A **segment** is part of a line. It has two end points.

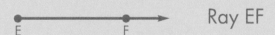 Segment AB

A **ray** has a line segment with only one end point. It goes on and on in the other direction.

Ray EF

An **angle** has two rays with the same end point.

Angle BAC

Directions: Write the name for each figure.

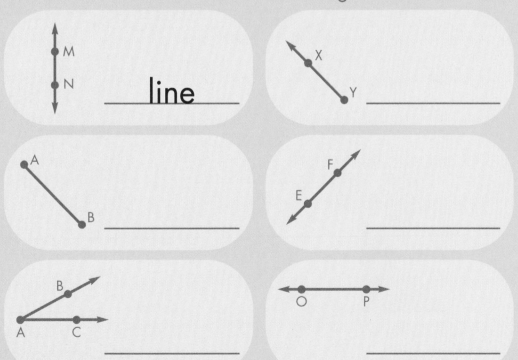

__line__

_____

_____   _____

_____   _____

Going the Distance

The perimeter is the distance around an object. Find the perimeter by adding the lengths of all the sides.

Directions: Find the perimeter for each object (ft. = feet).

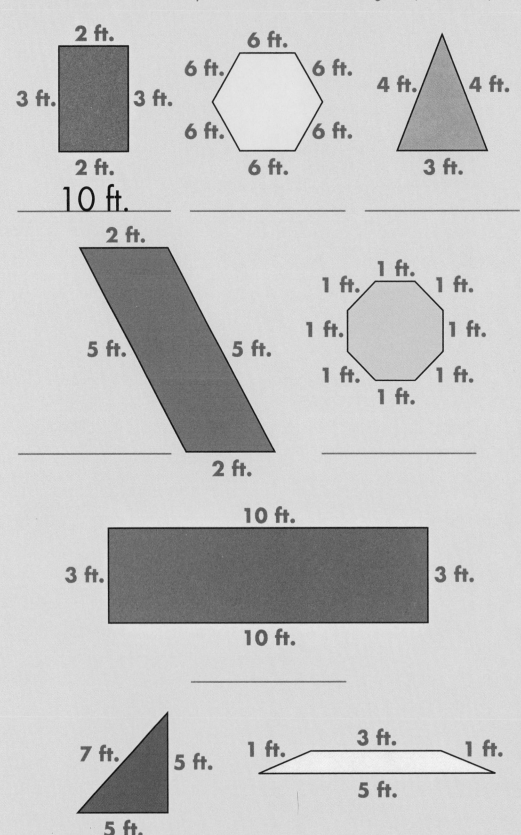

10 ft.

All Around Town

A **map scale** shows how far one place is from another. This map scale shows that 1 inch on this page equals 1 mile at the real location.

Directions: Use a ruler and the map scale to find out how far it is from Ann's house to other places. Round to the nearest mile.

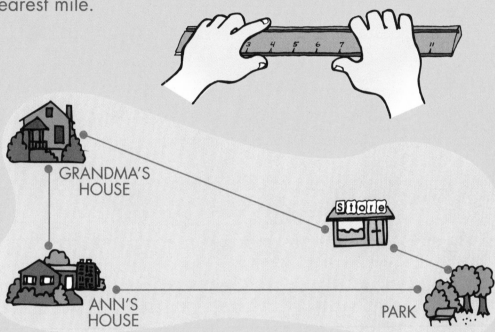

1. How far is it from Ann's house to the park?

   _____

2. How far is it from Ann's house to Grandma's house?

   _____

3. How far is it from Grandma's house to the store?

   _____

4. How far did Ann go when she went from her house to Grandma's and then to the store?

   _____

Blast Off!

Directions: Answer the questions about the graph.

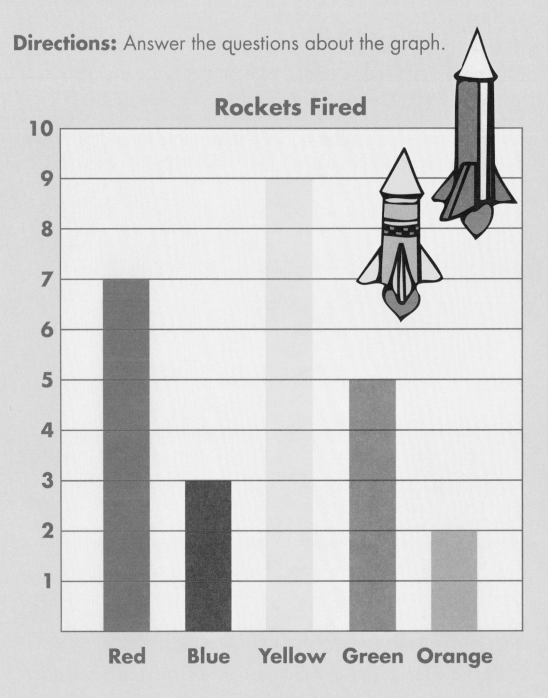

How many rockets did the Red Club fire? _7_

How many rockets did the Green Club fire? _5_

The Yellow Club fired 9 rockets. How many
more rockets did it fire than the Blue Club? _6_

How many rockets were fired in all? _26_

Weigh In

Ounces and pounds are measurements of weight in the standard measurement system. The ounce is used to measure the weight of very light objects. The pound is used to measure the weight of heavier objects. 16 ounces = 1 pound.

Example: 8 ounces   15 pounds

Directions: Decide if you would use ounces or pounds to measure the weight of each object. Circle your answer.

ounce   pound

ounce   pound

ounce   pound

ounce   pound

a chair: ounce   pound

a table: ounce   pound

a shoe: ounce   pound

a shirt: ounce   pound

Inching Along

An inch is a unit of length in the standard measurement system.

Directions: Use a ruler to measure each object to the nearest $\frac{1}{4}$ inch. Write **in.** to stand for inch.

Example:

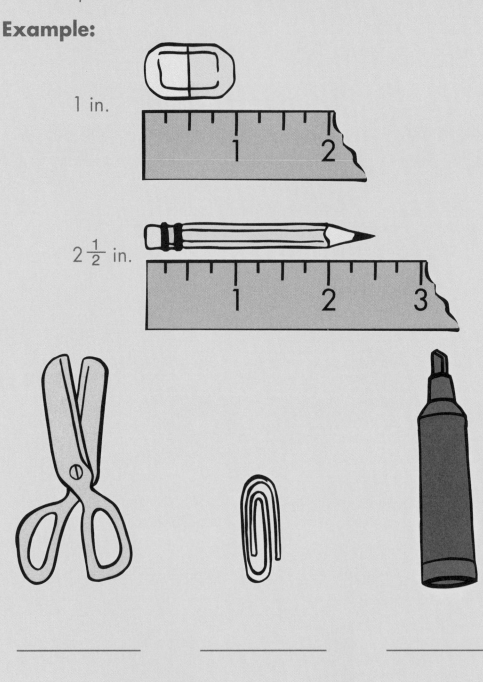

1 in.

$2\frac{1}{2}$ in.

_____   _____   _____

_____

_____

Centimeter Sense

A centimeter is a unit of length in the metric system. There are 2.54 centimeters in an inch.

Directions: Use a centimeter ruler to measure each object to the nearest half a centimeter. Write **cm** to stand for centimeter.

Example:

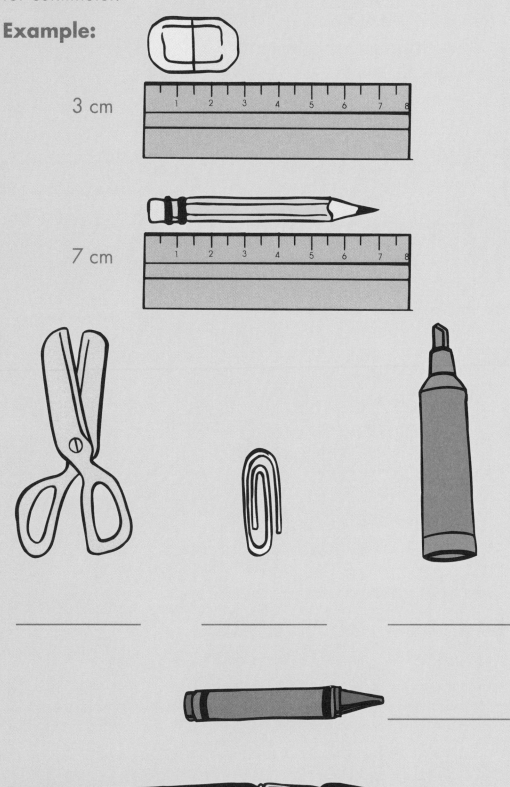

3 cm

7 cm

_____   _____   _____

_____

_____

Measuring Up:
Foot, Yard, Mile

Directions: Decide whether you would use foot, yard or mile to measure each object.

1 foot = 12 inches
1 yard = 36 inches or 3 feet
1 mile = 1,760 yards

length of a river _____ miles _____

height of a tree _____

width of a room _____

length of a football field _____

length of a dress _____

length of a race _____

width of a window _____

distance a plane travels _____

Directions: Solve the problem.

Tara races Tom in the 100-yard dash. Tara finishes 10 yards in front of Tom. How many feet did Tara finish in front of Tom?

_____

Measuring Up: Meter and Kilometer

Meters and kilometers are units of length in the metric system. A meter is equal to 39.37 inches. A kilometer is equal to about $\frac{5}{8}$ of a mile.

Directions: Decide whether you would use meter or kilometer to measure each object.

1 meter = 100 centimeters
1 kilometer = 1,000 meters

length of a river _____ **kilometer** _____

height of a tree _____

width of a room _____

length of a football field _____

length of a dress _____

length of a race _____

width of a window _____

distance a plane travels _____

Directions: Solve the problem.

Tara races Tom in the 100-meter dash.
Tara finishes 10 meters in front of Tom.
How many centimeters did Tara finish
in front of Tom? _____

Counting Back in Time

Another way to write numbers is to use Roman numerals.

I	1	VII	7
II	2	VIII	8
III	3	IX	9
IV	4	X	10
V	5	XI	11
VI	6	XII	12

Directions: Fill in the Roman numerals on the watch.

What time is it on the watch?

_____ o'clock

Do You Have the Time?

Directions: Write the time shown on each clock.

Example:

7:15   7:00

_____   _____   _____

_____   _____   _____

_____   _____   _____

From Dawn to Dark

In telling time, the hours between 12:00 midnight and 12:00 noon are a.m. hours. The hours between 12:00 noon and 12:00 midnight are p.m. hours.

Directions: Draw a line between the times that are the same.

Example:

7:30 in the morning — 7:30 a.m.

half-past seven a.m.

seven thirty in the morning

9:00 in the evening — 9:00 p.m.

nine o'clock at night

six o'clock in the evening	8:00 a.m.
3:30 a.m.	six o'clock in the morning
4:15 p.m.	6:00 p.m.
eight o'clock in the morning	eleven o'clock in the evening
quarter past five in the evening	three thirty in the morning
11:00 p.m.	four fifteen in the evening
6:00 a.m.	5:15 p.m.

Time Flies!

Directions: Add the hours and minutes together.
(Remember, 1 hour equals 60 minutes.)

Example:

2 hours 10 minutes
+ 1 hour 50 minutes
3 hours 60 minutes
        (1 hour)
4 hours

4 hours 20 minutes
+ 2 hours 10 minutes
6 hours 30 minutes

9 hours	1 hour	6 hours
+ 2 hours	+ 5 hours	+ 3 hours

6 hours 15 minutes   10 hours 30 minutes
+ 1 hour 15 minutes   + 1 hour 10 minutes

3 hours 40 minutes   11 hours 15 minutes
+ 8 hours 20 minutes   + 1 hour 30 minutes

4 hours 15 minutes   7 hours 10 minutes
+ 5 hours 45 minutes   + 1 hour 30 minutes

Taking Away Time

Directions: Subtract the hours and minutes. (Remember, 1 hour equals 60 minutes.) "Borrow" from the "hours" if you need to.

Example:

$$
\begin{array}{c}
5 \quad\quad 70 \\
\cancel{6}\ \text{hours}\ \cancel{10}\ \text{minutes} \\
-\ 2\ \text{hours}\ 30\ \text{minutes} \\
\hline
3\ \text{hours}\ 40\ \text{minutes}
\end{array}
$$

12 hours	5 hours	2 hours
– 2 hours	– 3 hours	– 1 hour

5 hours 30 minutes	9 hours 45 minutes
– 2 hours 15 minutes	– 3 hours 15 minutes

11 hours 50 minutes	12 hours
– 4 hours 35 minutes	– 6 hours 30 minutes

7 hours 15 minutes	8 hours 10 minutes
– 5 hours 30 minutes	– 4 hours 40 minutes

Money Matters

dollar = 100¢ or $1.00

 dime =
10¢ or $.10

 penny =
1¢ or $.01

 quarter =
25¢ or $.25

nickel =
5¢ or $.05

half-dollar =
50¢ or $.50

Directions: Write the amount for each group of money shown. Use a dollar sign and decimal point. The first one is done for you.

 **$.07**

 _____

 _____

 _____

 _____

 _____

Counting Cash

Directions: Write the amount for each group of money shown. Use a dollar sign and decimal point. The first one is done for you.

Five-dollar bill = 5 one dollar bills

Ten-dollar bill = 2 five-dollar bills or 10 one-dollar bills

$15.00 <u>   </u>

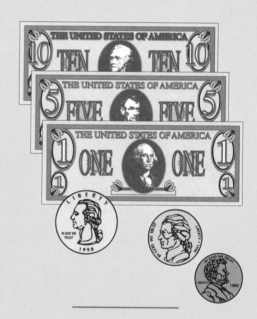

<u>   </u>   <u>   </u>

7 one-dollar bills, 2 quarters   <u>   </u>

2 five-dollar bills, 3 one-dollar bills, half-dollar   <u>   </u>

3 ten-dollar bills, 1 five-dollar bill, 3 quarters   <u>   </u>

Making Change

Directions: Subtract the money using decimals to show how much change a person would receive in each of the following.

Example:

Drew had 3 dollars. $3.00
He bought a baseball for $2.83.   −$2.83
How much change did he receive? $ .17

Paid 2 dollars.

_____

Paid 1 dollar.

_____

Paid 5 dollars.

_____

Paid 10 dollars.

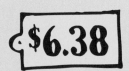

_____

Paid 4 dollars.

_____

Paid 7 dollars.

$6.38

_____

Fun Fair!

Directions: Read and solve each problem. The first one is done for you.

The clown started the day with 200 balloons. He gave away 128 of them. Some broke. At the end of the day he had 18 balloons left. How many of the balloons broke?   54

On Monday, there were 925 tickets sold to adults and 1,412 tickets sold to children. How many more children attended the fair than adults?   _____

At one game booth, prizes were given out for scoring 500 points in three attempts. Sanj scored 178 points on her first attempt, 149 points on her second attempt and 233 points on her third attempt. Did Sanj win a prize?   _____

The prize-winning steer weighed 2,348 pounds. The runner-up steer weighed 2,179 pounds. How much more did the prize steer weigh?   _____

Eat Your Veggies!

Directions: Read and solve each problem.

Jeff and Riley are planting a garden. They plant 3 rows of green beans with 8 plants in each row. How many green bean plants are there in the garden?

_____

There are 45 tomato plants in the garden. There are 5 rows of them. How many tomato plants are in each row?

_____

The children have 12 plants each of lettuce, broccoli and spinach. How many plants are there in all?

_____

Jeff planted 3 times as many cucumber plants as Riley. He planted 15 of them. How many did Riley plant?

_____

Riley planted 12 pepper plants. He planted twice as many green pepper plants as red pepper plants. How many green pepper plants are there?

_____

Farm Living

A fraction is a number that names part of a whole, such as $\frac{1}{2}$ or $\frac{1}{3}$.

Directions: Read and solve each problem.

There are 20 large animals on the Browns' farm. Two-fifths are horses, two-fifths are cows and the rest are pigs. Are there more pigs or cows on the farm?

_____

Farmer Brown had 40 eggs to sell. He sold half of them in the morning. In the afternoon, he sold half of what was left. How many eggs did Farmer Brown have at the end of the day?

_____

There is a fence running around seven-tenths of the farm. How much of the farm does not have a fence around it? Write the amount as a decimal.

_____

The Browns have 10 chickens. Two are roosters and the rest are hens. Write a decimal for the number that are roosters and for the number that are hens.

_____ roosters   _____ hens

A Race to the Finish

Directions: Read and solve each problem.

This year, hundreds of people ran in the
Capital City Marathon. The race is 4.2
kilometers long. When the first person crossed
the finish line, the last person was at the 3.7
kilometer point. How far ahead was the winner? _____

Hasaan crossed the finish line 10 meters ahead
of Lucy. Lucy was 5 meters ahead of Sam. How
far ahead of Sam was Hasaan? _____

Tony ran 320 yards from school to his home.
Then, he ran 290 yards to Jay's house. Together
Tony and Jay ran 545 yards to the store. How
many yards in all did Tony run? _____

The teacher measured the heights of three
children in her class. Gabriella was 51 inches
tall, Jimmy was 48 inches tall and Deepak was
$52\frac{1}{2}$ inches tall. How much taller is Deepak
than Gabriella? _____

Abbreviation: A shortened form of a word. Most abbreviations begin with a capital letter and end with a period. **Example:** Doctor = Dr.

Addition: "Putting together" or adding two or more numbers to find the sum.

Adjectives: Words that describe nouns. **Examples:** tall, four, cold, happy.

Adverbs: Words that describe verbs. They often tell how, when or where. **Examples:** here, today, quickly.

Alliteration: The repeated use of beginning sounds. They are also known as tongue twisters. **Example:** Peter Piper picked a peck of pickled peppers.

Alphabetical Order: Putting letters or words in the order in which they appear in the alphabet.

Analogy: A word pair which compares how things are related to each other.

Angle: Two rays with the same end point.

Antonyms: Words that are opposites. **Example:** hot and cold.

Apostrophes: Punctuation that is used with contractions in place of the missing letter or used to show ownership. **Examples:** don't, Susan's.

Articles: Small words that help us better understand nouns. **Examples:** a, an.

Biography: A type of nonfiction book written about a real person's life.

Capitalization: Letters that are used at the beginning of names of people, places, days, months and holidays. Capital letters are also used at the beginning of sentences.

Cause: The reason for an event.

Centimeter: A measurement of length in the metric system. There are 2.54 centimeters in an inch.

Cinquain: A five-line poem that follows the following form: Line 1: noun; Line 2: adjective, adjective; Line 3: verb + ing, verb + ing, verb + ing; Line 4: four-word phrase; Line 5: synonym for noun in line 1.

Classifying: Putting similar things into categories or groups.

Commands: Sentences that tell someone to do something. They usually begin with a verb or the word "please."

Commas: Punctuation marks which are used to separate words or phrases. They are also used to separate dates from years, cities from states, etc.

Common Nouns: Nouns that name any member of a group of people, places or things rather than specific people, places or things. **Example:** person.

Compare: To discuss how things are similar.

Compound Predicates: Two or more verbs that have the same subject.

Compound Sentences: Two complete ideas that are joined together into one sentence by a conjunction.

Compound Subject: Two or more nouns that have the same predicate.

Compound Word: Two words that are put together to make one new word. **Example:** base + ball = baseball.

Comprehension: Understanding what is seen, read or heard.

Consonants: Letters that are not vowels (every letter except a, e, i, o and u).

Contractions: Words that are a short way to write two words together. **Example:** isn't is short for is not.

Contrast: To discuss how things are different.

Coordinates: Points on a grid. They are named with numbers across, then down.

Decimal: A number with one or more places to the right of a decimal point, such as 6.5 or 3.78. Money amounts are written with two places to the right of a decimal point, such as $1.30.

Detail Sentence: A sentence in a paragraph that supports the main idea.

Dictionary Skills: Learning how to use a dictionary.

Difference: The answer in a subtraction problem.

Digit: The symbols used to write numbers: 0, 1, 2, 3, 4, 5, 6, 7, 8 and 9.

Directions: Sentences that are written as commands, telling someone to do something.

Dividend: The larger number that is divided by the smaller number, or divisor, in a division problem. In the problem 28 ÷ 7 = 4, 28 is the dividend.

Division: An operation to find out how many times one number is contained in another number. For example, 28 ÷ 4 = 7 means that there are seven groups of four in 28.

Divisor: The smaller number that is divided into the dividend in a division problem. In the problem 28 ÷ 7 = 4, 7 is the divisor.

Dollar: A dollar is equal to one hundred cents. It is written $1.00.

Drawing a Conclusion: Using clues to make a final decision about something.

Effect: What happens as a result of a cause.

Ending Sentences: Sentences at the end of a paragraph that tie the story together.

Entry Word: A word defined in a dictionary.

Exclamations: Sentences that express strong feelings. Exclamations often end with an exclamation point. These sentences can be short or long and can be a command. **Example:** Look at that!

Factors: The numbers multiplied together in a multiplication problem.

Fiction: A type of book about things that are made up or not true.

Following Directions: Doing what the directions say to do.

Fraction: A number that names part of a whole, such as $\frac{1}{2}$ or $\frac{2}{3}$.

Front-End Estimation: The process of using only the first digit in a number and replacing every other place value with a zero to round a number.

Future-Tense Verb: A verb that tells about something that has not happened yet but will happen in the future. "Will" or "shall" are usually used with future tense. **Example:** We will eat soon.

Geometry: The branch of mathematics that has to do with points, lines and shapes.

Graph: A drawing that shows information about numbers.

Guide Words: Words at the top of a dictionary page. They are the first and last words on that page.

Helping Verb: A word used with an action verb. **Example:** They are helping.

Homophones: Two words that sound the same but have different meanings and are usually spelled differently. **Example:** write and right.

Idiom: A saying in which the words do not mean exactly what they say.

Inference: Using logic to figure out what is not directly told.

Irregular Verbs: Verbs that do not change from the present tense to the past tense in the regular way with "d" or "ed." **Example:** run, ran.

Joining Words: Words that combine ideas in a sentence, such as "and," "but," "or," "because."

Kilometer: A measurement of distance in the metric system. There are 1,000 meters in a kilometer.

Library Skills: Learning how to use the library and its resources.

Line Segment: A part of a line with two end points.

Linking Verbs: Verbs that connect the noun to a descriptive word. Linking verbs are always a form of "to be." **Example:** I am tired.

Long Vowels: The letters a, e, i, o and u which say the "long" or letter name sound. Long a is the sound you hear in hay. Long e is the sound you hear in me. Long i is the sound you hear in pie. Long o is the sound you hear in no. Long u is the sound you hear in cute.

Making a Deduction: Using reasoning to arrive at a conclusion.

Main Idea: Finding the most important points. The main idea is what the story is mostly about.

Map Scale: Part of a map that shows how far one place is from another.

Meter: A measurement of length in the metric system. A meter is equal to 39.37 inches.

Middle Sentences: Sentences that support the topic sentence in a paragraph.

Mile: A measurement of distance in the standard measurement system. A mile is equal to 1,760 yards or 5,280 feet.

Multiple-Meaning Words: Words that are spelled the same but have different meanings or pronunciations, such as bow (ribbon) and bow (of a ship).

Multiplication: A short way to find the sum of adding the same number a certain amount of times. For example, 7 x 4 = 28 instead of 7 + 7 + 7 + 7 = 28.

Nonfiction: Writing based on facts. It usually gives information about people, places or things.

Nouns: Words that name a person, place or thing.

Ounce: A measurement of weight in the standard measurement system. There are 16 ounces in a pound.

Paragraphs: Groups of sentences that tell about the same thing.

Past-Tense Verb: A verb that tells about something that has already happened. A "d" or "ed" is usually added to the end of the word. **Example:** walked.

Percentage: The amount of a number out of 100. It uses the sign: %.

Perimeter: The distance around an object. Find the perimeter by adding the lengths of the sides.

Periodical: Writing that is printed regularly within a set period of time. **Example:** newspaper.

Phonics: Using the sound letters make to decode unknown words.

Place Value: The value of a digit, or numeral, shown by where it is in the number.

Plural Nouns: Nouns which name more than one person, place or thing.

Possessive Nouns: Nouns that tell who or what is the owner of something. **Example:** the dog's ball.

Possessive Pronouns: Pronouns that show ownership. **Example:** his dish.

Predicate: The verb in the sentence that tells the main action. It tells what the subject is doing, has done or will do.

Prefixes: Special word parts added to the beginnings of words. Prefixes change the meaning of words. **Example:** redo.

Prepositions: Words that show the relationship between a noun or pronoun and another word in the sentence. **Example:** The boy is behind the chair.

Present-Tense Verb: A verb that tells about something that is happening now, happens often or is about to happen. An "s" or "ing" is usually added to the verb. **Examples:** sings, singing.

Product: The answer of a multiplication problem.

Pronouns: Words that can be used in place of nouns. **Example:** it.

Proper Nouns: Nouns that name specific people, places or things. **Example:** Iowa.

Questions: Sentences that ask something. They begin with a capital letter and end with a question mark.

Quotation Marks: Punctuation marks that tell what is said by a person. Quotation marks go before and after a direct quote. **Example:** She said, "Here I am!"

Quotient: The answer of a division problem.

Ray: A line segment with only one end point. It goes on and on in the other direction.

Recalling Details: Being able to pick out and remember the who, what, when, where, why and how of what is read.

Reference Book: A book that tells basic facts. **Example:** a dictionary.

Regroup: To use ten ones to form one ten, ten tens to form 100, and so on.

Remainder: The number left over in the quotient of a division problem.

Rhymes: Words with the same ending sounds. **Example:** lake and cake.

Roman Numerals: Another way to write a number. The system uses Roman letters rather than standard digits.

Root Words: Words before a suffix or prefix is added. **Example:** Write is the root word of rewritten.

Rounding: Estimating a number by figuring a number using the closest "10" (or "100," "1,000," etc.).

Schedule: A chart with lists of times.

Sentences: A group of words that tell a complete idea, using a noun and a verb. They begin with a capital letter and have end punctuation (a period, question mark or exclamation point).

Sequencing: Putting words or events in a certain order.

Short Vowels: The letters a, e, i, o and u which say the short sound. Short a is the sound you hear in ant. Short e is the sound you hear in elephant. Short i is the sound you hear in igloo. Short o is the sound you hear in octopus. Short u is the sound you hear in umbrella.

Simple Predicate: The main verb of the predicate part of the sentence. **Example:** Dad will cook for us tonight. "Cook" is the simple predicate.

Simple Subject: The main noun in the complete subject part of the sentence. **Example:** The silly boy ran around. "Boy" is the simple subject.

Singular Nouns: Words that refer to only one thing.

Statements: Sentences that tell something. They begin with a capital letter and end with a period.

Subject: The noun that does the action. It tells who or what the sentence is about. A noun or pronoun will always be part of the subject.

Subtraction: "Taking away" or subtracting one number from another to find the difference.

Suffixes: Word parts added to the end of a word to change or add to its meaning. **Example:** statement.

Syllable: Word parts. Each syllable has one vowel sound.

Synonyms: Words that mean the same or nearly the same. **Example:** small and little.

Topic Sentence: Usually the first sentence in a paragraph. The topic sentence tells what the story is about.

Venn Diagram: A chart that shows comparisons and contrasts.

Verbs: The action words in a sentence. The word that tells what something does or that something exists. **Examples:** run, is.

Vowels: The letters a, e, i, o, u and sometimes y.

Word Order: The logical order of words in a sentence.

Yard: A measurement of distance in the standard measurement system. There are 3 feet in a yard.

Addition, Subtraction, Multiplication, Division

Have your child compute his/her age in years, in months and in days. Then, try your age!

Purchase a blank book or notebook to serve as your child's Math Journal. As you complete math pages together, your child can write his/her reflections about what he/she has learned. If your child wants, you can write comments to him/her in the book to give your child positive feedback and reinforce the skill learned.

Talk with your child about how math is used in your profession. Make a list of other occupations, and talk about how math is used in these professions as well.

Imagine that "National Math Day" has become a holiday. Ask your child: If you were in charge of the celebration, what "Math Events" would you plan?

Adjectives

Blindfold your child so he/she can touch, smell and hear but cannot see. Seal a scoop of ice cream in a plastic bag. Hand the bag to your child to touch without opening the bag. Ask your child to describe the ice cream using several adjectives. Write down your child's words. Repeat this activity with other objects which allow your child to describe what he/she can see, hear, smell, touch or taste.

Alphabetical Order

Alphabetical order is a skill used every day. Have your child look up phone numbers or find videos at the local video store. (Note: Not all stores arrange their movies alphabetically.)

Antonyms/Synonyms/Homophones

If you notice your child using a homophone incorrectly in his/her writing ("there" for "their"), make sure to correct him/her before it becomes a habit.

As your child communicates in writing or speech, he/she will need to increase his/her vocabulary. Many words are overused and can be replaced with synonyms. Challenge your child to think of words that could replace over-used ones: "I'm thinking of a word that means the same as . . . ." Then, have your child try to challenge you.

Have your child write a list of antonym word pairs, such as light, dark; silent, noisy; neat, sloppy; etc. Encourage him/her to use a variety of words. The list should contain about 10–12 word pairs. With this list, help your child make an Antonym Tree. Have on hand scissors, glue, some colored markers or crayons and several sheets of construction paper of different sizes and colors. Have your child cut out a tree trunk and branches and glue them onto large white background paper. Cut out leaves of various colors. Your child can then print the antonym pairs on the different leaves and glue them onto the tree branches. Synonym or homophone pairs could also be used.

Compound Words

Give your child a section of the newspaper. Ask him/her to find and circle as many compound words as possible. This could also be done with other parts of speech, such as adjectives, verbs, pronouns, etc.

Comprehension

While cause-effect relationships are learned in real-life situations—e.g., if I touch the hot stove, I will burn my hand—those same cause-effect relationships in reading are not as easy to see. Present a situation, such as "All the food in the freezer has thawed." Ask your child to think of possible causes for the occurrence. Then, give your child practice imagining effects. "Jim wrecked his bicycle. What happened next?"

At this age, your child is or may soon be reading "chapter books." These books have very few pictures. Check your child's comprehension by having him/her draw pictures representing the action or the problem for each chapter. Before starting each new chapter, ask your child to predict what will happen.

As you read with your child, encourage him/her to picture in his/her mind what is happening. This will help your child recall the story using the "mind's eye" as well as the ear. Ask him/her to retell the story, noting details from the beginning, middle and end.

When you read with your child, take turns asking each other questions about the story. Your child may find it more difficult to think of a question to ask than to answer a question, so give him/her clues from the story to help.

Invite your child to write a different ending or new chapter to a story. If your child can do this in a logical manner, he/she has grasped the plot or ideas presented.

Encourage your child to become a "thinker." Use the activities and lessons in this book as a springboard for related lessons. As you work with your child on classifying, for example, you are helping him/her develop the skills needed to determine the main idea and details. Give your child a group of words and ask him/her to tell you the category in which they belong. Your child should also be able to look at a group of three to four words and decide which word does not belong. As your child writes, help him/her use these skills to group related sentences into good paragraphs. Discuss whether a book is fiction or nonfiction. Guide your child to understand the difference and to read a variety of literature. If your child is able to place story events in the proper sequence, he/she probably understands the events of the story. Name an event from the story and ask if it happened near the beginning, middle or end.

Save the Sunday comics and cut out strips with interesting pictures or ones that tell a simple story. Cut the frames apart and challenge your child to reorder the story. Take this a step further by suggesting that your child create an extra frame to show what might happen next. For another activity, cut out or cover the text in the speech balloons and challenge your child to create a story that fits the pictures.

Details

Write ideas on index cards, such as summer vacation. Then, invite your child to write three or four details about the idea, such as lots of fun, no school, playing with friends, camping, riding bikes, and so on.

Write a simple sentence for your child. **Example:** The cat ran down the street. Show your child how adding details makes the sentence more interesting. **Example:** The fluffy white cat ran quickly down the quiet street.

Take this idea one step further and have your child write a story about a family trip or a day at the mall, the beach or at Grandma's. Encourage him/her to include lots of details about what happened.

Place some items on a table and give your child 10 to 30 seconds to memorize them. Then, as your child's back is turned, remove one of the items. Have your child see if he/she can tell you what is missing. Increase the difficulty by removing two or more items.

Dictionary Skills

Dictionary skills will be used more and more often as your child progresses through school, so encourage him/her to become familiar with this resource. Don't look up a word for your child but assist if he/she asks for your help. Play dictionary games with your child. Time your child to see how quickly he/she can look up a word or see who can open up the dictionary closer to the page on which a given word is found.

Following Directions

Your child may find it difficult to understand oral directions. This usually happens because he/she is not "really" listening. Make sure you have eye contact and the full attention of your child when giving directions.

Check out a book on origami, the ancient art of Japanese paper-folding. Challenge your child to read the directions to create figures from paper.

Encourage your child to follow directions with fun activities like scavenger hunts, mazes and puzzles. Ask your child to help with recipes and have him/her follow the directions given on boxes from your cupboard or freezer.

Written directions need to be understood before they can be followed. Check his/her understanding before he/she attempts an activity.

Show your child the importance of following directions by preparing a simple recipe together. Point out how the steps must be followed in order. Then, invite him/her to write a recipe for making a sandwich, chocolate milk or another simple food. Encourage your child to include all the necessary steps, then see if you can create the recipe from your child's directions.

Inference

Guide your child to "figure out" what an author means even when it is not stated directly. Practice by describing a situation to your child and having him/her tell you what is happening.
Example: I got some baby shampoo and a big towel. I went outside, got the hose and turned on the water. The dog took one look at me and tried to run out the gate. What is happening? (I am getting ready to wash the dog.)

Main Idea

Set up a group of items and have your child locate something else that would fit in that group. You may want to provide several items from which he/she can choose. As your child's skill level increases, invite him/her to locate something on his/her own.

Invite your child to group things into categories such as color, shape, size or idea to see if the concept, or main idea, is understood. **Examples:** round things, wild animals, sports played outside, board games.

Ask your child questions while reading together, such as "What is the most important thing the author is saying in this paragraph?"

Money

Talk with your child about different things he/she can do to earn money.

Pose this question to your child: If we did not have money, what would we use to buy things? Tell your child about the Native American system of using wampum as "money." Do research together about other monetary systems.

Quotation Marks

From the newspaper, cut out your child's favorite comic strip. Have your child rewrite the comic strip conversations, using sentences with quotation marks. Check your child's sentences for proper use of quotation marks and discuss what you find with your child.

Reading

Read to and with your child, and let him/her see you reading for enjoyment. Encourage your child to read for enjoyment and make sure to provide many opportunities for your child to discuss what he/she is reading.

Ask your child: What if you couldn't read? Challenge him/her to make a list of as many kinds of reading as he/she thinks he/she does in a day. Then, together keep track of every time you use reading throughout the day—reading directions on packages while cooking dinner, reading road signs, looking up information in a telephone book, reading mail, etc. Your child will be impressed by the important role reading plays in your lives!

When your child finishes a book, create fun ways to share the information in the book with you or with a friend. Some ways to do this might be to have your child write a letter from one character to another, create a comic strip illustrating the events of the book or write a journal entry one of the characters might write.

Before you take your child to a movie or buy a new video, suggest that your child read the book first, or read it aloud to him/her. Talk with your child about the similarities and differences between the book and the movie and discuss which he/she likes better and why.

Encourage your child to dress up as a character from one of his/her favorite books and to act out events from the book for members of your family.

Encourage your child to keep a "reading log" of books he/she has read, and write his/her reflections about each book. After your child has read several books, challenge him/her to go through the journal and classify the book titles by genre. Add symbols to indicate the types of books your child has read: F for fiction and N for nonfiction. To make this activity more challenging, further extend these classifications, indicating M for mystery, B for biography, P for poetry, etc.

When you vacation with your child, purchase postcards from the various locations you visit. Let your child write important information about your trip on the postcards. Use a hole punch to make a hole in each postcard and fasten them together for a unique travel memory book!

Make sure your child has a current library card and plan a weekly time to visit the library together. Each time, take a few moments to teach your child about different parts of the library. For example, on one visit, you can show him/her where fiction and nonfiction books are located. Regular library visits will help you to expose your child to many genres of books and help him/her to develop a life-long love of learning.

Spelling

Review with your child how to study a word:

1) Look at the word.
2) Say the word.
3) Write the word.
4) Check yourself.

Repeat the steps if the word is incorrect.

Every day, write one sentence with errors in it. Have your child correct it. Focus on spelling, punctuation, capitalization and word order. **Example:** the dag and cat fite.

Help your child create his/her own spelling dictionary.

Discuss the origins of words with your child. Latin and Greek influences are most common. For example, "cent" in money or "century" means 100 and comes from the Latin word centum. Many dictionaries list word origins.

Teach your child more words with multiple meanings using a dictionary.

Other things to do besides write a word for practice:

- Chant the spelling.
- Write the word in the air.
- Use frosting or a condiment to write the word on food.
- Fill an empty mustard container with water and write the words on your sidewalk or driveway.
- Write the word in the snow with a stick or umbrella.
- Put the word to a song (i.e., sing the tune of "Bingo" for a 5-letter word).
- Spell the word aloud, tapping on consonants, clapping on vowels.

Have a word poster or folder for your child to keep a list of new words. Then, he/she can study and review the words independently.

Play charades with your child using spelling words. Each guess must be spelled out.

Subjects and Predicates

Give your child 20 index cards. He/she should write ten subjects on the first ten cards, and ten predicates on the remaining cards. Punch holes in the upper right-hand corner of each stack and fasten with a notebook ring. Have your child flip through the stack of cards, mixing subjects and predicates to form a variety of sentences.

Time

Talk with your child about different methods of keeping time, such as with clocks, stopwatches, calendars, etc. Let your child make a list of as many ways to keep time as he/she can.

Have your child time how long it takes the family to eat dinner. Have him/her write down the start time and the stop time, and subtract.

Have your child make a "time management" chart to plan his/her time from after school until bedtime.

Verbs

Write some action verbs, such as run, talk, jump, watch, read, wave, drive, slide, bend, etc., on paper. Put the pieces of paper into a hat or can. Let your child choose a piece of paper and pantomime the word for you to guess. Take turns doing this until you've both had several turns.

Writing

Review the Writing Process:

1) prewriting and brainstorming
2) first (or rough) draft
3) revision
4) proofreading
5) publish final edited copy

Encourage your child to write in a daily journal. Provide a spiral notebook with wide-spaced lines. Journal entries are usually anecdotal and personal. Encourage your child to ask questions, describe dreams or write accounts of his/her day in the journal. Following are some suggestions for journal starters:

I'd like to go . . .	I want to know more about . . .
My birthday is . . .	Did you know . . .
Sometimes I feel . . .	My favorite . . .
I laughed and laughed . . .	My best friend is . . .
I went to . . .	When I got to the party, . . .
I felt silly . . .	Was I ever mad when . . .
I really miss . . .	I feel _____ when . . .
I try hard to . . .	Last night when I went to bed . . .
I can't wait until . . .	I felt so proud when . . .

Encourage your child to compose poems, copying the patterns of the following poetry:

Couplet (a two-line rhyme)
Example: I saw a cloud way up high,
Soaring gently in the sky.

Limerick (a humorous poem that has the rhyme scheme AABBA)
Example: There was a young man from Maine (A)
Who liked to stand out in the rain. (A)
Although he's all wet, (B)
He's standing there yet. (B)
That crazy young man from Maine. (A)

Quatrain (a four-line poem with rhymes AABB or ABAB)
Examples:

AABB	ABAB
I asked a small boy, (A)	As I watched a waterfall, (A)
Who played with a toy, (A)	Water splashed upon my face. (B)
Why trees do not rain. (B)	Although I was quite small, (A)
He could not explain. (B)	I knew it was a grand place. (B)

224

---

8 — My Story

READING

Directions: Fill in the blanks. Use these sentences to write a story about yourself.

Answers will vary.

I feel happy when _____

I feel sad when _____

I am good at _____

Words that describe me: _____ _____

_____ _____ _____

I can help at home by _____

_____

My friends like me because _____

_____

I like to _____

_____

My favorite food is _____

My favorite animal is _____

Now . . . take your answers and write a story about **you!**

---

9 — Without a Sound

READING

Some words are more difficult to read because they have one or more silent letters. Many words you already know are like this.

Examples: w**ro**ng and ni**gh**t.

Directions: Circle the silent letters in each word. The first one is done for you.

w(r)ong	an(sw)er	autum(n)	(wh)ole
(k)nife	(h)our	(w)rap	com(b)
si(gh)t	strai(gh)t	(k)nee	(k)nown
lam(b)	tau(gh)t	s(c)ent	dau(gh)ter

Directions: Draw a line between the rhyming words. The first one is done for you.

knew — try
sees — boat
taut — stone
wrote — true
comb — song
straight — trees
sigh — home
known — great
wrong — caught

---

10 — The Long and Short of It

READING

In some word "families," the vowels have a long sound when you would expect them to have a short sound. For example, the i has a short sound in **chill**, but a long sound in **child**. The o has a short sound in **cost**, but a long sound in **most**.

Directions: Read the words in the box below. Write the words that have a long vowel sound under the word **LONG**, and the words that have a short vowel sound under the word **SHORT**. (Remember, a long vowel says its name—like **a** in **ate**.)

old	odd	gosh	gold	sold
soft	toast	frost	lost	most
doll	roll	bone	done	kin
mill	mild	wild	blink	blind

LONG
bone
old
roll
most
gold
sold
toast
mild
wild
blind

SHORT
doll
odd
gosh
done
kin
soft
mill
frost
lost
blink

---

11 — F Is for Fun!

READING

Sometimes letters make sounds you don't expect. Two consonants can work together to make the sound of one consonant. The **f** sound can be made by **ph**, as in the word **elephant**. The consonants **gh** are most often silent, as in the words **night** and **though**. But they also can make the **f** sound as in the word **laugh**.

Directions: Circle the letters that make the f sound. Write the correct word from the box to complete each sentence.

ele(ph)ant	cou(gh)	tele(ph)one	dol(ph)ins
enou(gh)	tou(gh)	al(ph)abet	rou(gh)

1. The **dolphins** were playing in the sea.
2. Did you have __enough__ time to do your homework?
3. A cold can make you __cough__ and sneeze.
4. The __elephant__ ate peanuts with his trunk.
5. The road to my school is __rough__ and bumpy.
6. You had a __telephone__ call this morning.
7. The __tough__ meat was hard to chew.
8. The __alphabet__ has 26 letters in it.

---

12 — Give Me a Break!

READING

All words can be divided into syllables. Syllables are word parts which have one vowel sound in each part.

Directions: Draw a line between the syllable part and write the word on the correct line below. The first one is done for you.

lit·tle	bum·ble·bee	pil·low
truck	daz·zle	dog
pen·cil	flag	an·gel·ic
re·joic·ing	ant	tel·e·phone

1 SYLLABLE
truck
flag
ant
dog

2 SYLLABLES
little
pencil
dazzle
pillow

3 SYLLABLES
re joicing
bumblebee
angelic
telephone

---

13 — Razzle Dazzle

READING

When the letters **le** come at the end of a word, they sometimes have the sound of **ul**, as in raffle.

Directions: Draw a line to match the syllables so they make words. The first one is done for you.

can — gle
tur — cle
pur — ple
cir — kle
spar — zle
raf — dle
ea — fle
siz — tle

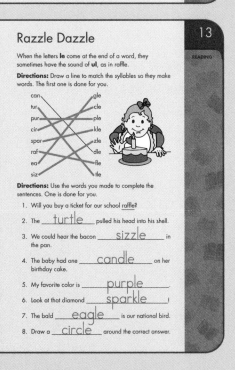

Directions: Use the words you made to complete the sentences. One is done for you.

1. Will you buy a ticket for our school raffle?
2. The __turtle__ pulled his head into his shell.
3. We could hear the bacon __sizzle__ in the pan.
4. The baby had one __candle__ on her birthday cake.
5. My favorite color is __purple__
6. Look at that diamond __sparkle__!
7. The bald __eagle__ is our national bird.
8. Draw a __circle__ around the correct answer.

14 — It Takes Two

A compound word is two small words put together to make one new word. Compound words are usually divided into syllables between the two words.

Directions: Read the words. Then, divide them into syllables. The first one is done for you.

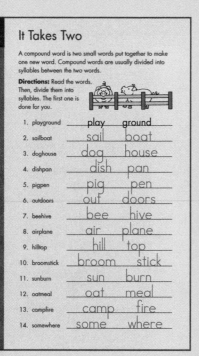

1. playground — play / ground
2. sailboat — sail / boat
3. doghouse — dog / house
4. dishpan — dish / pan
5. pigpen — pig / pen
6. outdoors — out / doors
7. beehive — bee / hive
8. airplane — air / plane
9. hilltop — hill / top
10. broomstick — broom / stick
11. sunburn — sun / burn
12. oatmeal — oat / meal
13. campfire — camp / fire
14. somewhere — some / where

15 — Two in One

Directions: Read the compound words in the word box. Then use them to answer the questions. The first one is done for you.

sailboat	blueberry	bookcase	beehive
dishpan	pigpen	classroom	broomstick
treetop	fireplace	newspaper	sunburn

Which compound word means . . .

1. a case for books? — bookcase
2. a berry that is blue? — blueberry
3. a hive for bees? — beehive
4. a place for fires? — fireplace
5. a pen for pigs? — pigpen
6. a room for a class? — classroom
7. a pan for dishes? — dishpan
8. a boat to sail? — sailboat
9. a paper for news? — newspaper
10. a burn from the sun? — sunburn
11. the top of a tree? — treetop
12. a stick for a broom? — broomstick

16 — Play Ball!

Many words have more than one meaning. These words are called **multiple-meaning words**. Think of how the word is used in a sentence or story to determine the correct meaning.

Directions: The following baseball words have multiple meanings. Write the correct word in each baseball below.

play   bat   ball   fly   run

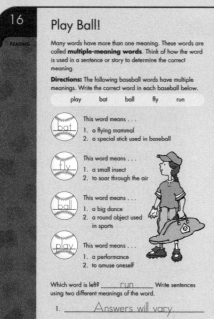

bat — This word means . . .
1. a flying mammal
2. a special stick used in baseball

fly — This word means . . .
1. a small insect
2. to soar through the air

ball — This word means . . .
1. a big dance
2. a round object used in sports

play — This word means . . .
1. a performance
2. to amuse oneself

Which word is left? **run** Write sentences using two different meanings of the word.

1. Answers will vary
2. _____

17 — Up to Bat

Directions: Complete each sentence using one of the words below.

bank   ball   park   run
play   kid   fly   bat

1. The kitten watched the **fly** crawl slowly up the wall.
2. "You wouldn't **kid** me, would you?" asked Dad.
3. Do you think Aunt Donna and Uncle Mike will come to my school **play**?
4. He hit the ball so hard it broke the **bat**.
5. "My favorite part of the story is when the princess goes to the **ball**," sighed Veronica.
6. My brother scored the first **run** in the game.

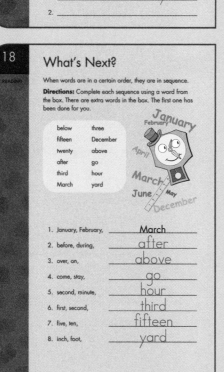

18 — What's Next?

When words are in a certain order, they are in sequence.

Directions: Complete each sequence using a word from the box. There are extra words in the box. The first one has been done for you.

below	three
fifteen	December
twenty	above
after	go
third	hour
March	yard

1. January, February, **March**
2. before, during, **after**
3. over, on, **above**
4. come, stay, **go**
5. second, minute, **hour**
6. first, second, **third**
7. five, ten, **fifteen**
8. inch, foot, **yard**

19 — Order, Order!

Directions: Fill in the blank spaces with what comes next in the series. The first one is done for you.

year	large	sixth	Wednesday
twenty	mile	night	paragraph
February	winter	seventeen	

1. Sunday, Monday, Tuesday, **Wednesday**
2. third, fourth, fifth, **sixth**
3. November, December, January, **February**
4. tiny, small, medium, **large**
5. fourteen, fifteen, sixteen, **seventeen**
6. morning, afternoon, evening, **night**
7. inch, foot, yard, **mile**
8. day, week, month, **year**
9. spring, summer, autumn, **winter**
10. five, ten, fifteen, **twenty**
11. letter, word, sentence, **paragraph**

20 — What Happened?

Directions: Read each story. Circle the phrase that tells what happened before.

1. Anya is very happy now that she has someone to play with. She hopes that her new sister will grow up quickly!

   A few days ago . . .
   Anya was sick.
   (Anya's mother had a baby.)
   Anya got a new puppy.

2. Sara tried to mend the tear. She used a needle and thread to sew up the hole.

   While playing, Sara had . . .
   broken her bicycle.
   lost her watch.
   (torn her shirt.)

3. The movers took Diego's bike off the truck and put it in the garage. Next, they moved his bed into his new bedroom.

   Diego's family . . .
   (bought a new house.)
   went on vacation.
   bought a new truck.

4. Katie picked out a book about dinosaurs. Conner, who likes sports, chose two books about baseball.

   Katie and Conner . . .
   (went to the library.)
   went to the playground.
   went to the grocery store.

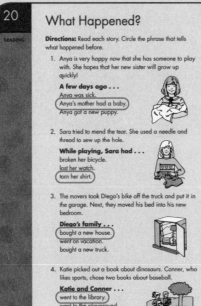

21 — Tell Me a Story

Directions: Number these sentences from 1 to 5 to show the correct order of the story.

Building a Treehouse

4 They had a beautiful treehouse!
2 They got wood and nails.
1 Jay and Lisa planned to build a treehouse.
5 Now, they like to eat lunch in their treehouse.
3 Lisa and Jay worked in the backyard for three days building the treehouse.

A School Play

5 Everyone clapped when the curtain closed.
4 The girl who played Snow White came onto the stage.
2 All the other school children went to the gym to see the play.
3 The stage curtain opened.
1 The third grade was going to put on a play about Snow White.

22 — House Hunt

Directions: Learning to follow directions is very important. Use the map to find your way to different houses.

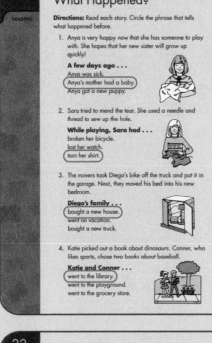

1. Color the start house yellow.
2. Go north 2 houses, and east two houses.
3. Go north 2 houses, and west 4 houses.
4. Color the house green.
5. Start at the yellow house.
6. Go east 1 house, and north 3 houses.
7. Go west 3 houses, and south 3 houses.
8. Color the house blue.

North
West ←→ East
South

23 — Super Salad

Following directions means doing what the directions say to do. Following directions is an important skill to know. When you are trying to find a new place, build a model airplane or use a recipe, you should follow the directions given.

Directions: Read the following recipe. Then, answer the questions on page 24.

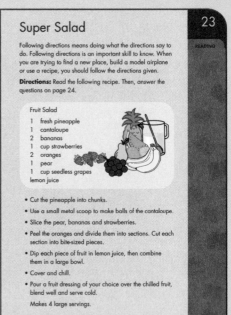

Fruit Salad
1 fresh pineapple
1 cantaloupe
2 bananas
1 cup strawberries
2 oranges
1 pear
1 cup seedless grapes
lemon juice

- Cut the pineapple into chunks.
- Use a small metal scoop to make balls of the cantaloupe.
- Slice the pear, bananas and strawberries.
- Peel the oranges and divide them into sections. Cut each section into bite-sized pieces.
- Dip each piece of fruit in lemon juice, then combine them in a large bowl.
- Cover and chill.
- Pour a fruit dressing of your choice over the chilled fruit, blend well and serve cold.

  Makes 4 large servings.

24 — Super Salad

Directions: Using the recipe on page 23, answer the questions below.

1. How many bananas does this recipe require? __2__

2. Does the recipe explain why you must dip the fruit in lemon juice? __no__

   Why would it be important to do this? It keeps the fruit from turning brown quickly

3. Would your fruit salad be as good if you did not cut the pineapple or section the oranges? Why or why not?

   No because it would be harder to eat such big chunks of food

4. Which do you do first? (Check one.)

   ___ Pour dressing over the fruit.
   ✓ Slice the pear.
   ___ Serve the fruit salad.

5. Which three fruits do you slice?

   pear
   bananas
   strawberries

25 — Shy Giants

Directions: Read about the giant panda. Then, answer the questions.

Giant pandas are among the world's favorite animals. They look like big, cuddly stuffed toys. There are not very many pandas left in the world. You may have to travel a long way to see one.

The only place on Earth where pandas live in the wild is in the bamboo forests of the mountains of China. It is hard to see pandas in the forest because they are very shy. They hide among the many bamboo trees. It also is hard to see pandas because there are so few of them. Scientists think there may be less than 1,000 pandas living in the mountains of China.

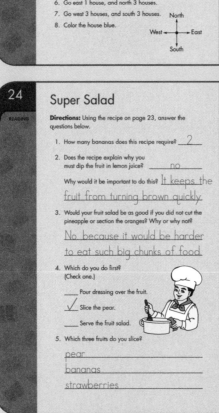

1. Write a sentence that tells the main idea of this story:

   There are very few pandas left in the world

2. What are two reasons that it is hard to see pandas in the wild?

   1) They hide among the bamboo trees
   2) There are very few pandas

3. How many pandas are believed to be living in the mountains of China?

   fewer than 1,000

26 — A Man of Many Talents

Directions: Read about Thomas Jefferson. Then, answer the questions.

Thomas Jefferson was the third president of the United States. He was also an inventor. That means he created things that had never been made before. Thomas Jefferson had many inventions. He built a chair that rotated in circles. He created a rotating music stand. He also made a walking stick that unfolded into a chair. Thomas Jefferson even invented a new kind of plow for farming.

1. The main idea is: (Circle one.)

Thomas Jefferson was very busy when he was president.

(Thomas Jefferson was a president and an inventor.)

2. What do we call a person who has new ideas and makes things that no one else has made before?

   __an inventor__

3. List three of Thomas Jefferson's inventions.

   1) _Answers will vary_

   2) _____

   3) _____

27 — Riding Through History

Directions: Read about the bicycle. Then, answer the questions.

One of the first bicycles was made out of wood. It was created in 1790 by an inventor in France. The first bicycle had no pedals. It looked like a horse on wheels. The person who rode the bicycle had to push it with his/her legs. Pedals weren't invented until nearly 50 years later.

Bikes became quite popular in the United States during the 1890s. Streets and parks were filled with people riding them. But those bicycles were still different from the bikes we ride today. They had heavier tires, and the brakes and lights weren't very good. Bicycling is still very popular in the United States. It is a great form of exercise and a handy means of transportation.

1. Who invented the bicycle? _an inventor in France_

2. What did it look like? _no pedals, wooden_
   looked like a horse on wheels

3. When did bikes become popular in the United States?
   during the 1890's

4. Where did people ride bikes? _streets and parks_

5. How is biking good for you? _good for exercise_

6. How many years have bikes been popular in the
   United States? _109 years_

28 — The Peaceful Pueblos

Directions: Read about the Pueblo Native Americans. Then, answer the questions.

The Pueblo (pooh-eb-low) Native Americans live in the southwestern United States in New Mexico and Arizona. They have lived there for hundreds of years. The Pueblos have always been peaceful Native Americans. They never started wars. They only fought if attacked first.

The Pueblos love to dance. Even their dances are peaceful. They dance to ask the gods for rain or sunshine. They dance for other reasons, too. Sometimes the Pueblos wear masks when they dance.

1. The main idea is: (Circle one.)

(Pueblos are peaceful Native Americans who still live in parts of the United States.)

Pueblo Native Americans never started wars.

2. Do Pueblos like to fight? _No_

3. What do the Pueblos like to do? _They love_
   to dance

29 — All About Adobe

Directions: Read about adobe houses. Then, answer the questions.

Pueblo Native Americans live in houses made of clay. They are called adobe (ah-doe-bee) houses. Adobe is a yellow-colored clay that comes from the ground. The hot sun in New Mexico and Arizona helps dry the clay to make strong bricks. The Pueblos have used adobe to build their homes for many years.

Pueblos use adobe for other purposes, too. The women in the tribes make beautiful pottery out of adobe. While the clay is still damp, they form it into shapes. After they have made the bowls and other containers, they paint them with lovely designs.

1. What is the subject of this story?
   adobe

2. Who uses clay to make their houses?
   Pueblo Native Americans

3. How long have they been building adobe houses?
   many years

4. Why do adobe bricks need to be dried?
   to make the clay bricks strong

30 — Discover the Details

Directions: Read the story. Then, answer the questions.

Thomas Edison was one of America's greatest inventors. An inventor thinks up new machines and new ways of doing things. Edison was born in Milan, Ohio in 1847. He went to school for only three months. His teacher thought he was not very smart because he asked so many questions.

Edison liked to experiment. He had many wonderful ideas. He invented the light bulb and the phonograph (record player).

Thomas Edison died in 1931, but we still use many of his inventions today.

1. What is an inventor?
   A person who thinks up new
   machines and new ways of
   doing things

2. Where was Thomas Edison born?
   Milan, Ohio

3. How long did he go to school?
   three months

4. What are two of Edison's inventions?
   the light bulb and the phonograph

31 — Panda Life

Directions: Read the story. Then, answer the questions.

Giant pandas do not live in families like people do. The only pandas that live together are mothers and their babies. Newborn pandas are very tiny and helpless. They weigh only five ounces when they are born—about the weight of a stick of butter! They are born with their eyes closed, and they have no teeth.

It takes about three years for a panda to grow up. When full grown, a giant panda weighs about 300 pounds and is five to six feet tall. Once a panda is grown up, it leaves its mother and goes off to live by itself.

1. What pandas live together?
   mothers and their babies

2. How much do pandas weigh when they are born?
   about five ounces

3. Why do newborn pandas live with their mothers?
   They are very tiny and helpless

4. When is a panda full grown?
   at three years old

32 Seeing Hsing-Hsing

Inference is using logic to figure out what is not directly told.

Directions: Read the story. Then, answer the questions.

In the past, many thousands of people went to the National Zoo each year to see Hsing-Hsing, the panda. Sometimes, there were as many as 1,000 visitors in one hour! Like all pandas, Hsing-Hsing spent most of his time sleeping. Because pandas are so rare, most people think it is exciting to see even a sleeping panda!

1. Popular means well-liked. Do you think giant pandas are popular?

   Yes

2. What clue do you have that pandas are popular?

   They had as many as 1,000 visitors an hour

3. What did most visitors see Hsing-Hsing doing?

   sleeping

33 Got the Message?

Directions: Read the messages on the memo board. Then, answer the questions.

1. What kind of lesson does Katie have?

   dance

2. What time is Amy's birthday party? 1:00 p.m

3. What kind of appointment does Jeff have on September 3rd? doctor

4. Who goes to choir practice? mom

5. Where is Dad's meeting?

   fire station

34 All in Order

Dictionaries contain meanings and pronunciations of words. The words in a dictionary are listed in alphabetical order. Guide words appear at the top of each dictionary page. They help us know at a glance what words are on each page.

Directions: Place the words in alphabetical order.

APPLE	CRAB	CRIB	FROG
apple	cake	crib	ear
atlas	coat	dog	egg
book	crab	drip	frog

apple	dog	crab	ear
book	atlas	cake	frog
egg	drip	coat	crib

35 Did You Hear the News?

A newspaper has many parts. Some of the parts of a newspaper are:

- banner — the name of the paper
- lead story — the top news item
- caption — sentences under the picture which give information about the picture
- sports — scores and information on current sports events
- comics — drawings that tell funny stories
- editorial — an article by the editor expressing an opinion about something
- ads — paid advertisements
- weather — information about the weather
- advice column — letters from readers asking for help with a problem
- movie guides — a list of movies and movie times
- obituary — information about people who have died

Directions: Match the newspaper sections below with their definitions.

banner — the name of the paper
lead story — the top news item
caption — sentences under pictures
editorial — an article by the editor
movies — movies and movie times
obituary — information about people who have died

36 Right on Schedule!

Here is a schedule for the day's activities at Camp Do-A-Lot. Amira and Jessie need help to decide what they will do on their last day.

Directions: Use this schedule to answer the questions on page 37.

CAMP DO-A-LOT
Saturday

Breakfast	6:30 A.M.	Dining Hall
Archery	7:30 A.M.	Field behind the Hall
Canoeing	7:30 A.M.	Blue Bottom Lake
Landscape Painting	7:30 A.M.	Rainbow Craft Shed
Horseback Riding	8:45 A.M.	Red Barn
Landscape Painting	8:45 A.M.	Rainbow Craft Shed
Scavenger Hunt	8:45 A.M.	Dining Hall
Cabin Clean-up	10:45 A.M.	Assigned Cabins
Lunch	11:45 A.M.	Dining Hall
Canoeing	1:00 P.M.	Blue Bottom Lake
Archery	1:00 P.M.	Field behind the Hall
Scavenger Hunt	1:00 P.M.	Dining Hall
Awards Ceremony	2:45 P.M.	Outdoor Theater
Dismissal	3:30 P.M.	

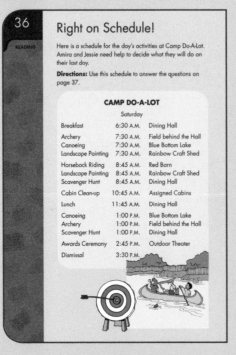

37 Right on Schedule!

Directions: Use the schedule of activities on page 36 to answer the questions.

1. Where do Amira and Jessie need to go to take part in archery?

   the field behind the Dining Hall

2. Both girls want to go canoeing. What are the two times that canoeing is offered?

   7:30 a.m and 1:00 p.m

3. Amira and Jessie love to go on scavenger hunts. They agree to go on the hunt at 1:00 P.M. When will they have to go canoeing?

   7:30 a.m

4. Only one activity on the last day of camp takes place at the Outdoor Theater. What is it?

   The Awards Ceremony

Pretend you are at Camp Do-A-Lot with Amira and Jessie. On the line next to each time, write which activity you would choose to do.

7:30 A.M. _____ Answers will vary

8:45 A.M. _____

1:00 P.M. _____

38 — Get Real!

Something that is **real** could actually happen. Something that is **fantasy** is not real. It could not happen.

Examples: Real: Dogs can bark.
Fantasy: Dogs can fly.

Directions: Look at the sentences below. Write **real** or **fantasy** next to each sentence.

1. My cat can talk to me. _fantasy_
2. Witches ride brooms and cast spells. _fantasy_
3. Dad can mow the lawn. _real_
4. I ride a magic carpet to school. _fantasy_
5. I have a man-eating tree. _fantasy_
6. My sandbox has toys in it. _real_
7. Mom can bake chocolate chip cookies. _real_
8. Mark's garden has tomatoes and corn in it. _real_

Write your own real sentence.
Answers will vary.

Write your own fantasy sentence.
Answers will vary.

39 — Introducing Idioms

Idioms are a colorful way of saying something ordinary. The words in idioms do not mean exactly what they say.

Directions: Read the idioms listed below. Draw a picture of the literal meaning. Then, match the idiom to its correct meaning.

Pictures will vary.

Jump on the bandwagon! — Get involved!
She eats like a bird. — She doesn't eat very much.
Don't cry over spilled milk! — Don't worry about things that have already happened.
Don't let the cat out of the bag! — Keep the secret.
You are the apple of my eye. — I think you are special.

40 — All in the Family

Analogies compare how things are related to each other.
Directions: Complete the other analogies.
Example: Finger is to **hand** as **toe** is to **foot**.

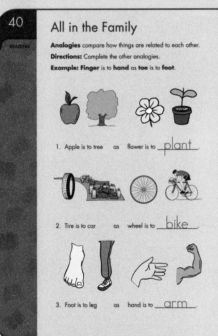

1. Apple is to tree as flower is to _plant_.
2. Tire is to car as wheel is to _bike_.
3. Foot is to leg as hand is to _arm_.

41 — Awesome Analogies

Directions: Complete each analogy using a word from the box. The first one has been done for you.

week   bottom   month   tiny   sentence   out   eye

1. **Up** is to **down** as **in** is to _out_
2. **Minute** is to **hour** as **day** is to _week_
3. **Month** is to **year** as **week** is to _month_
4. **Over** is to **under** as **top** is to _bottom_
5. **Big** is to **little** as **giant** is to _tiny_
6. **Sound** is to **ear** as **sight** is to _eye_
7. **Page** is to **book** as **word** is to _sentence_

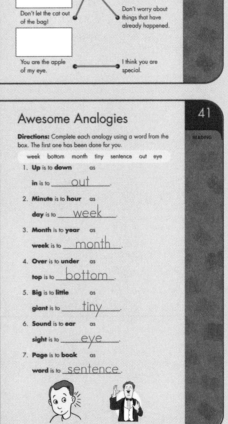

42 — In the Garden

Directions: Write each word from the box in the correct category.

robin	elm	buckeye	willow
sunflower	bluejay	canary	oak
rose	wren	tulip	morning glory

Trees
buckeye
elm
willow
oak

Birds
robin
canary
bluejay
wren

Flowers
sunflower
rose
tulip
morning glory

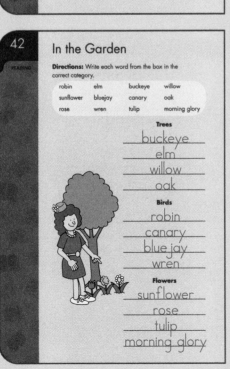

43 — Find the Kind

Directions: Write the word from the word box that tells what kinds of things are in each sentence.

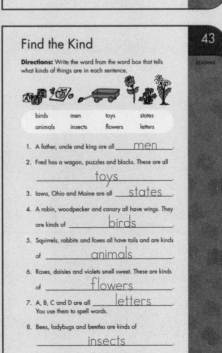

| birds | men | toys | states |
| animals | insects | flowers | letters |

1. A father, uncle and king are all _men_.
2. Fred has a wagon, puzzles and blocks. These are all _toys_
3. Iowa, Ohio and Maine are all _states_
4. A robin, woodpecker and canary all have wings. They are kinds of _birds_
5. Squirrels, rabbits and foxes all have tails and are kinds of _animals_
6. Roses, daisies and violets smell sweet. These are kinds of _flowers_
7. A, B, C and D are all _letters_ You use them to spell words.
8. Bees, ladybugs and beetles are kinds of _insects_

44 Bookshelf Basics

A **fiction** book is a book about things that are made up or not true. Fantasy books are fiction. A **nonfiction** book is about things that have really happened. Books can be classified into more types:

Mystery – books that have clues that lead to solving a problem or mystery

Biography – book about a real person's life

Poetry – a collection of poems, which may or may not rhyme

Fantasy – books about things that cannot really happen

Sports – books about different sports or sport figures

Travel – books about going to other places

Directions: Write mystery, biography, poetry, fantasy, sports or travel next to each title.

The Life of Helen Keller	biography
Let's Go to Mexico!	travel
The Case of the Missing Doll	mystery
How to Play Golf	sports
Turtle Soup and Other Poems	poetry
Fred's Flying Saucer	fantasy

45 Real or Fantasy?

Directions: Read the paragraphs below. Determine whether each paragraph is fiction or nonfiction. Circle the letter **F** for fiction or the letter **N** for nonfiction.

Megan and Mariah skipped out to the playground. They enjoyed playing together at recess. Today, it was Mariah's turn to choose what they would do first. To Megan's surprise, Mariah asked, "What do you want to do, Megan? I'm going to let you pick since it's your birthday!" (**F**) **N**

It is easy to tell an insect from a spider. An insect has three body parts and six legs. A spider has eight legs and no wings. Of course, if you see the creature spinning a web, you will know what it is. An insect wouldn't want to get too close to the web or it would be stuck. It might become dinner! **F** (**N**)

My name is Lee Chang, and I live in a country that you call China. My home is on the other side of the world from yours. When the sun is rising in my country, it is setting in yours. When it is day at your home, it is night at mine. **F** (**N**)

46 Author ABCs

Ms. Ling, the school librarian, needs help shelving books. Fiction titles are arranged in alphabetical order by the author's last name. Ms. Ling has done the first set for you.

3 Silverstein, Shel

1 Bridwell, Norman

2 Farley, Walter

Directions: Number the following groups of authors in alphabetical order.

2	Bemelmans, Ludwig	**4**	Perkins, Al
4	Stein, R.L.	**2**	Dobbs, Rose
3	Sawyer, Ruth	**1**	Baldwin, James
1	Baum, L. Frank	**3**	Kipling, Rudyard

The content of some books is also arranged alphabetically.

Directions: Circle the books that are arranged in alphabetical order.

T.V. guide   dictionary   encyclopedia   novel
almanac   science book   Yellow Pages   catalog

Write the books you circled in alphabetical order.

1. dictionary
2. encyclopedia
3. Yellow Pages

47 Pick a Periodical

Libraries also have periodicals such as magazines and newspapers. They are called **periodicals** because they are printed regularly within a set period of time. There are many kinds of magazines. Some discuss the news. Others cover fitness, cats or other topics of special interest. Almost every city or town has a newspaper. Newspapers usually are printed daily, weekly or even monthly. Newspapers cover what is happening in your town and in the world. They usually include sections on sports and entertainment. They present a lot of information. Answers will vary.

Directions: Follow the instructions.

1. Choose an interesting magazine. What is the name of the magazine? _____

   List the titles of three articles in the magazine.

   _____
   _____
   _____

2. Now, look at a newspaper. What is the name of the newspaper? _____

   The title of a newspaper story is called a headline. What are some of the headlines in your local newspaper?

   _____
   _____
   _____

48 City Kids

Directions: Look for similarities and differences in the following paragraphs. Then, answer the questions.

Phong and Chris both live in the city. They live in the same apartment building and go to the same school. Phong and Chris sometimes walk to school together. If it is raining or storming, Phong's dad drives them to school on his way to work. In the summer, they spend a lot of time at the park across the street from their building.

Phong lives in Apartment 12-A with his little sister and mom and dad. He has a collection of model race cars that he put together with his dad's help. He even has a bookshelf full of books about race cars and race car drivers.

Chris has a big family. He has two older brothers and one older sister. When Chris has time to do anything he wants, he gets out his butterfly collection. He notes the place he found each specimen and the day he found it. He also likes to play with puzzles.

1. Compare Phong and Chris. List at least three similarities.

They both live in the city. Phong and Chris spend a lot of time at the park. They go to the same school.

2. Contrast Phong and Chris. List two differences.

Phong has a little sister; Chris has two brothers and one sister. Chris has a butterfly collection; Phong collects model race cars.

49 Taking Flight

Directions: List the similarities and differences you find below on a chart called a **Venn diagram**. This kind of chart shows comparisons and contrasts.

Butterflies and moths belong to the same group of insects. They both have two pairs of wings. Their wings are covered with tiny scales. Both butterflies and moths undergo metamorphosis, or a change, in their lives. They begin their lives as caterpillars.

1. Both have two pairs of wings. Their wings are covered with tiny scales. Both begin their lives as caterpillars.

2. Butterflies fly during the day; moths fly at night. Butterflies' bodies are slender and hairless; moths', plump and furry. Butterflies land wings up and moths land wings spread out.

Moths	**Both**	**Butterflies**
Fly at night	2 pairs of wings	Fly during the day
Plump furry body	Wings have tiny scales	Slender hairless body
Land wings spread out	Have been caterpillers	Land wings straight up

50 For a Good Cause

A **cause** is the reason for an event. An **effect** is what happens as a result of a cause.

Directions: Circle the cause and underline the effect in each sentence. They may be in any order. The first one has been done for you.

1. (The truck hit an icy patch) and skidded off the road.

2. (When the door slammed shut) the baby woke up crying.

3. Our soccer game was cancelled (when) (it began to storm)

4. Dad and Mom are adding a room onto the house (since our family is growing)

5. (Our car ran out of gas on the way to town,) so we had to walk.

6. (The home run in the ninth inning) helped our team win the game.

7. We had to climb the stairs (because the elevator was broken)

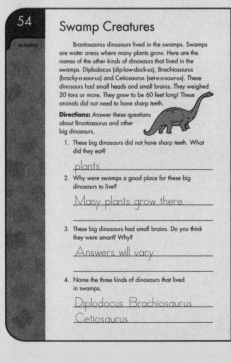

51 Searching for Clues

Cause and effect sentences often use clue words to show the relationship between two events. Common clue words are **because, so, when** and **since**.

Directions: Read the sentences below. Circle each clue word. The first one has been done for you.

1. I'll help you clean your room, (so) we can go out to play sooner.

2. (Because) of the heavy snowfall, school was closed today.

3. She was not smiling, (so) her mother wanted her school pictures taken again.

4. Mrs. Wilderman came to school with crutches today, (because) she had a skating accident.

5. (When) the team began making too many mistakes at practice, the coach told them to take a break.

52 Action . . . Reaction!

Directions: Draw a line to match each phrase to form a logical cause and effect sentence.

1. Dad gets paid today, so — because she is sick.

2. When the electricity went out, — we're going out for dinner.

3. Courtney can't spend the night — we grabbed the flashlights.

4. Our front window shattered — when the baseball hit it.

Directions: Read each sentence beginning. Choose an ending from the box that makes sense. Write the correct letter on the line.

1. Her arm was in a cast, because   C

2. They are building a new house on our street, so   A

3. Since I'd always wanted a puppy,   D

4. I had to renew my library book,   B

A. we all went down to watch.
B. since I hadn't finished it.
C. she fell when she was skating.
D. Mom gave me one for my birthday.

53 Get Ready For Robots

Directions: Read the story. Then, answer the questions.

There are many different kinds of robots. One special kind of robot takes the place of people in guiding airplanes and ships. They are called "automatic pilots." These robots are really computers programmed to do just one special job. They have the information to control the speed and direction of the plane or ship.

Robots are used for many jobs in which a person can't get too close because of danger, such as in exploding a bomb. Robots can be controlled from a distance. This is called "remote control." These robots are very important in studying space. In the future, robots will be used to work on space stations and on other planets.

1. The main idea of this story is:
   Robots are used for many different jobs.

2. Why are robots good in dangerous jobs?
   They are machines. They can't be hurt the way people can.

3. What is "remote control"?
   controlled from a distance

4. What will robots be used for in the future?
   to work on space stations and on other planets

5. What would you have a robot do for you?
   Answers will vary

54 Swamp Creatures

Brontosaurus dinosaurs lived in the swamps. Swamps are water areas where many plants grow. Here are the names of the other kinds of dinosaurs that lived in the swamps. Diplodocus (dip-low-dock-us), Brachiosaurus (bracky-o-saur-us) and Cetiosaurus (set-e-o-saur-us). These dinosaurs had small heads and small brains. They weighed 20 tons or more. They grew to be 60 feet long! These animals did not need to have sharp teeth.

Directions: Answer these questions about Brontosaurus and other big dinosaurs.

1. These big dinosaurs did not have sharp teeth. What did they eat?
   plants

2. Why were swamps a good place for these big dinosaurs to live?
   Many plants grow there.

3. These big dinosaurs had small brains. Do you think they were smart? Why?
   Answers will vary

4. Name the three kinds of dinosaurs that lived in swamps.
   Diplodocus Brachiosaurus Cetiosaurus

55 The Frilly Lizard

Triceratops was one of the last dinosaurs to develop. It lived in the Cretaceous (kre-tay-shus) period of history. It was in this time that the dinosaurs became extinct. Triceratops means "three-horned lizard." It was a strong dinosaur and able to defend itself well since it lived during the same time period as Tyrannosaurus Rex.

Triceratops was a plant-eating dinosaur. Its body was 20 feet long, and its head, including the three horns and bony "frill," was another $6\frac{1}{2}$ feet.

Directions: Answer these questions about Triceratops.

1. Dinosaurs became extinct during the Cretaceous period of history.

2. What does **Triceratops** mean?
   three-horned lizard

3. What information above tells you that Triceratops was able to defend itself?
   It was strong; it lived at the same time as Tyrannosaurus Rex; it had three horns and a bony frill.

232

ANSWER KEY

56

Dino Tracks

Dinosaurs roamed the Earth for 125 million years. Can you imagine that much time? About 40 years ago, some people found fossils of dinosaur tracks in Connecticut. Fossils are rocks that hold the hardened bones, eggs and footprints of animals that lived long ago. The fossil tracks showed that many dinosaurs walked together in herds. The fossils showed more than 2,000 dinosaur tracks!

Directions: Answer these questions about fossils.

1. What did the people find in the fossils?

   dinosaur tracks

2. In what state were the fossils found?

   Connecticut

3. How many tracks were in the fossils?

   more than 2,000 tracks

4. What did the tracks show?

   that many dinosaurs walked together in herds

5. How long did dinosaurs roam the Earth?

   125 million years

57

Model Mania

Some people can build models of dinosaurs. The models are fakes, of course. But they are life-size and they look real! The people who build them must know the dinosaur inside and out. First, they build a skeleton. Then, they cover it with fake "skin." Then, they paint it. Some models have motors in them. The motors can make the dinosaur's head or tail move. Have you ever seen a life-size model of a dinosaur?

Directions: Answer these questions about dinosaur models.

1. Circle the main idea:

   Some models of dinosaurs have motors in them.

   (Some people can build life-size models of dinosaurs that look real.)

2. What do the motors in model dinosaurs do?

   The motors can make the dinosaur's head or tail move

3. What is the first step in making a model dinosaur?

   build a skeleton

4. Why do dinosaur models look real?

   They have skin and move like real dinosaurs

58

Growing Up . . . and Up and Up!

Kareem Abdul-Jabbar grew up to be more than 7 feet tall! Kareem's father and mother were both very tall. When he was 9 years old, Kareem was already 5 feet 4 inches tall. Kareem was raised in New York City. He went to Power Memorial High School and played basketball on that team. He went to college at UCLA. He played basketball in college, too. At UCLA, Kareem's team lost only two games in 3 years! After college, Kareem made his living playing basketball.

Directions: Answer these questions about Kareem Abdul-Jabbar.

1. Who is the story about?

   Kareem Abdul-Jabbar

2. For what is this athlete famous?

   playing basketball

3. When did Kareem reach the height of 5 feet 4 inches?

   when he was 9 years old

4. Where did Kareem go to college?

   UCLA

5. Why did Kareem grow so tall?

   His father and mother were both very tall

59

Small but Mighty

Mary Lou Retton became the first U.S. woman to win Olympic gold in gymnastics. She accomplished this at the 1984 Olympics held in Los Angeles, when she was 16 years old. "Small but mighty" would certainly describe this gymnast.

She was the youngest of five children—all good athletes. She grew up in Fairmont, West Virginia, and began her gymnastic training at the age of 7.

Most women gymnasts are graceful, but Mary Lou helped open up the field of gymnastics to strong, athletic women. Mary Lou was 4 feet 10 inches tall and weighed a mere 95 pounds!

Directions: Answer these questions about Mary Lou Retton.

1. Circle the main idea:

   Mary Lou loved performing.

   (Mary Lou is a famous Olympic gymnast.)

2. She was born in Fairmont, West Virginia

3. At what age did she begin her gymnastics training?

   7 years old

4. Mary Lou won a gold medal when she was 16 years old.

60

Journey to a New Frontier

In 1801, President Thomas Jefferson chose an army officer named Meriwether Lewis to lead an expedition through our country's "new frontier." He knew Lewis would not be able to make the journey by himself, so he chose William Clark to travel with him. The two men had known each other in the army. They decided to be co-leaders of the expedition.

The two men and a group of about 45 others made the trip from the state of Missouri, across the Rocky Mountains all the way to the Pacific Coast. They were careful in choosing the men who would travel with them. They wanted men who were strong and knew a lot about the wilderness. It was also important that they knew some of the Native American languages.

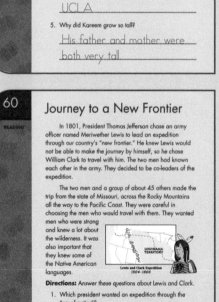

Lewis and Clark Expedition 1804–1806

Directions: Answer these questions about Lewis and Clark.

1. Which president wanted an expedition through the "new frontier"?

   Thomas Jefferson

2. Look at a United States map or a globe. In what direction did Lewis and Clark travel? (Circle one.)

   north   south   east   (west)

3. About how many people made up the entire expedition, including Lewis and Clark?

   47 people

61

Trials of the Trail

Lewis and Clark and their men had seen large grizzly bears as they traveled through the West. They were thankful they had their weapons with them. But meeting the grizzlies was not the hardest part of the journey. It was also hard to cross the Rocky Mountains. It took the explorers and their "party" a month to make this part of their trip. The friendly Shoshone tribe was very helpful in telling them how they could cross the mountains.

There were many reasons why this part of the trip was difficult. The steep, narrow pathways sometimes caused the horses to fall over the cliffs to their deaths. Many times the men had to lead the horses. There were fewer wild animals for the men to hunt for food.

Directions: Answer these questions about the hardships of the expedition.

1. What was the hardest part of the trip?

   crossing the Rocky Mountains

2. Lewis and Clark got help from which friendly Native American tribe?

   the Shoshone tribe

3. What word in the story means "a group of people traveling together"?

   party

4. What caused some of the horses to fall to their deaths?

   the steep, narrow pathways in the Rocky Mountains

62 — The Thief of Sherwood Forest

Long ago in England there lived a man named Robin Hood. Robin lived with a group of other men in the woods. These woods were called Sherwood Forest.

Robin Hood was a thief—a different kind of thief. He stole from the rich and gave what he stole to the poor. Poor people did not need to worry about going into Sherwood Forest. In fact, Robin Hood often gave them money. Rich people were told to beware. If you were rich, would you stay out of Sherwood Forest?

Directions: Answer these questions about Robin Hood.

1. What was the name of the woods where Robin Hood lived?

   Sherwood Forest

2. What did Robin Hood do for a living?

   He was a thief

3. What was different about Robin Hood?

   He stole from the rich and gave to the poor.

4. Did poor people worry about going into Sherwood Forest? Why or why not?

   No. Because Robin Hood wouldn't steal from them.

5. Do you think rich people worried about going into Sherwood Forest? Why?

   Yes. Because Robin Hood might steal from them.

63 — Robin Hood and the King

Everyone in England knew about Robin Hood. The king was mad! He did not want a thief to be a hero. He sent his men to Sherwood Forest to catch Robin Hood. But they could not catch him. Robin Hood outsmarted the king's men every time!

One day, Robin Hood sent a message to the king. The message said, "Come with five brave men. We will see who is stronger." The king decided to fool Robin Hood. He wanted to see if what people said about Robin Hood was true. The king dressed as a monk. A monk is a poor man who serves God. Then, he went to Sherwood Forest to see Robin Hood.

Directions: Circle the correct answer to these questions about the king's meeting with Robin Hood.

1. If the stories about Robin Hood were true, what happened when the king met Robin Hood?

   Robin Hood robbed the king and took all his money.

   (Robin Hood helped the king because he thought he was a poor man.)

2. Why didn't the king want Robin Hood to know who he was?

   He was afraid of Robin Hood.

   (He wanted to find out what Robin Hood was really like.)

3. Why couldn't the king's men find Robin Hood?

   (Robin Hood outsmarted them.)

   They didn't look in Sherwood Forest.

64 — Robin Hood and the King

The king liked Robin Hood. He said, "Here is a man who likes a good joke." He told Robin Hood who he really was. Robin Hood was not mad. He laughed and laughed. The king invited Robin Hood to come and live in the castle. The castle was 20 miles away. Robin had to walk south, cross a river and make two left turns to get there. He stayed inside the castle grounds for a year and a day.

Then, Robin grew restless and asked the king for permission to leave. The king did not want him to go. He said Robin Hood could visit Sherwood Forest for only one week. Robin said he missed his men but promised to return. The king knew Robin Hood never broke his promises.

Directions: Answer these questions about Robin Hood and the king.

1. Do you think Robin Hood returned to the castle? yes

2. Why do you think Robin Hood laughed when the king told him the truth?

   because he enjoyed a good joke

3. Give directions from Sherwood Forest to the king's castle.

   Walk south, cross a river and make two left turns.

4. Circle the main idea:

   (The king liked Robin Hood, but Robin missed his life in Sherwood Forest.)

   Robin Hood thought the castle was boring.

65 — Crazy for Catnip!

Do you have a cat? Do you have catnip growing around your home? If you don't know, your cat probably does. Cats love the catnip plant and can be seen rolling around in it. Some cat toys have catnip inside them because cats love it so much.

People can enjoy catnip, too. Some people make catnip tea with the leaves of the plant. It is like the mint with which people make tea.

Another refreshing drink can be made with the berries of the sumac bush or tree. Native Americans would pick the red berries, crush them and add water to make a thirst-quenching drink. The berries were sour, but they must have believed that the cool, tart drink was refreshing. Does this remind you of lemonade?

Directions: Answer these questions about unusual plants.

1. What is the main idea of the first two paragraphs above?

   Cats and people can both enjoy catnip

2. Write two ways cats show that they love catnip.

   1) by rolling around in it

   2) by playing with a catnip toy

3. How can people use catnip?

   They can make tea with it.

66 — The Greenest Place on Earth

The soil in rainforests is very dark and rich. The trees and plants that grow there are very green. People who have seen one say a rainforest is "the greenest place on Earth." Why? Because it rains a lot. With so much rain, the plants stay very green. The earth stays very wet. Rainforests cover only 6 percent of the Earth. But they are home to 66 percent of all the different kinds of plants and animals on Earth! Today, rainforests are threatened by such things as acid rain from factory smoke emissions around the world and from farm expansion. Farmers living near rainforests cut down many trees each year to clear the land for farming.

Directions: Answer these questions about rainforests.

1. What do the plants and trees in a rainforest look like?

   They are very green.

2. What is the soil like in a rainforest?

   very dark and rich

3. How much of the Earth is covered by rainforests?

   6 percent

4. What percentage of the Earth's plants and animals live there?

   66 percent

67 — The Kinkajou

If you have ever seen a raccoon holding its food by its "hands" and carefully eating it, you would have an idea of how the kinkajou (king-kuh-joo) eats. This animal of the rainforest is a "cousin" of the raccoon. Unlike its North American cousin, though, it is a golden-brown color.

The kinkajou's head and body are 17 to 22 inches long. The long tail of the kinkajou comes in handy for hanging around its neighborhood! It weighs very little—about 5 pounds. (You may have a 5-pound bag of sugar or flour in your kitchen to help you get an idea of the kinkajou's weight.)

This rainforest animal eats a variety of things. It enjoys nectar from the many rainforest flowers, insects, fruit, honey, birds and other small animals. Because it lives mostly in the trees, the kinkajou has a ready supply of food.

Directions: Answer these questions about the kinkajou.

1. The kinkajou is a "cousin" to the raccoon

2. Do you weigh more or less than the kinkajou? more

   Answers will vary but may include:

   1) nectar

   2) insects

   3) fruit

68 A Trip to the Rainforest

Many people travel to the rainforest each year. Some go by car, some go by train and some go by school bus! You don't even need a passport—the only thing you need is a field-trip permission slip.

If you are lucky enough to live in the Cleveland, Ohio area, you might get to take a class trip to the rainforest there. It is next to the Cleveland Zoo. This "rainforest" is a building that contains all the sights, sounds, smells and temperatures of the real rainforest. You will get to see many of the animals, big and small, that you could see if you went to Central or South America. The plants that grow there also grow in the rainforest. It is an interesting way to get an idea of what life is like in that part of the world!

Directions: Answer these questions about visiting the "rainforest."

1. If you lived in northern Ohio, name three ways you could get to the "rainforest."

   by car, train or school bus

2. In this "rainforest" you can see animals and plants that are found in the real rainforest.

3. Do you think it would be hot or cold in this "rainforest" building?

   (hot) cold

4. The real rainforest is located in both Central America and South America.

69 Not Just Any Cat

The jaguar weighs between 100 and 250 pounds. It can be as long as 6 feet! This is not your ordinary house cat!

One strange feature of the jaguar is its living arrangements. The jaguar has its own territory. No other jaguar lives in its "home range." It would be very unusual for one jaguar to meet another in the rainforest. One way they mark their territory is by scratching trees.

Have you ever seen your pet cat hide in the grass and carefully and quietly sneak up on an unsuspecting grasshopper or mouse? Like its gentler, smaller "cousin," the jaguar stalks its prey in the high grass. It likes to eat small animals, such as rodents, but can attack and kill larger animals such as tapirs, deer and cattle. It is good at catching fish as well.

Directions: Answer these questions about the jaguar.

1. The jaguar lives:
   a. in large groups
   (b.) alone
   c. under water

2. This large cat marks its territory by:
   a. black marker
   b. roaring
   (c.) scratching trees

3. What does the jaguar eat? small animals, tapirs, deer and cattle

4. How much does it weigh? between 100 and 250 pounds

70 Out of This World

There are eight planets in our solar system. All of them circle the Sun. The planet closest to the Sun is named Mercury. The Romans said Mercury was the messenger of the gods. The second planet from the Sun is named Venus. Venus shines the brightest. Venus was the Roman goddess of beauty. Earth is the third planet from the Sun. It is about the same size as Venus. After Earth is Mars, which is named after the Roman god of war. The other four planets are Jupiter, Saturn, Uranus, and Neptune. They, too, are named after Roman gods.

Directions: Answer these questions about our solar system.

1. How many planets are in our solar system?
   8

2. What do the planets circle?
   the Sun

3. What are the planets named after?
   Roman gods and goddesses

4. Which planet is closest to the Sun?
   Mercury

5. Which planet is about the same size as Earth?
   Venus

71 A Visit to Venus

For many years, no one knew much about Venus. When people looked through telescopes, they could not see past Venus' clouds. Long ago, people thought the clouds covered living things. Spacecraft radar has shown this is not true. Venus is too hot for life to exist. The temperature on Venus is about 900 degrees! Remember how hot you were the last time it was 90 degrees? Now imagine it being 10 times hotter. Nothing could exist in that heat. It is also very dry on Venus. For life to exist, water must be present. Because of the heat and dryness, we know there are no people, plants or other life on Venus.

Directions: Answer these questions about Venus.

1. Circle the main idea:
   We cannot see past Venus' clouds to know what the planet is like.
   (Spacecraft radar shows it is too hot and dry for life to exist on Venus.)

2. What is the temperature on Venus? 900 degrees

3. This temperature is how many times hotter than a hot day on Earth?
   6 times hotter
   (10 times hotter)

4. In the past, why did people think life might exist on Venus?
   They couldn't see past the clouds.

72 Welcome to Earth!

One planet in our solar system certainly supports life—Earth. Our planet is the third planet from the Sun and takes 365 days, or 1 year, to orbit the Sun. This rotation makes it possible for most of our planet to have four seasons—winter, spring, summer and fall.

Besides being able to support life, our planet is unique in another way—Earth is 75% covered by water. No other planet has that much, if any, liquid on its surface. This liquid and its evaporation help provide the cloud cover and our climate patterns.

Earth has one natural satellite—the Moon. Scientists and other experts all over the world have created and sent into orbit other satellites used for a variety of purposes—communication, weather forecasting, and so on.

Directions: Answer these questions about Earth.

1. How much of Earth is covered by water? 75%

2. The Moon is a natural satellite of Earth.

3. How long does it take Earth to orbit the Sun?
   365 days or 1 year

4. How does water make Earth the "living planet"?
   Its evaporation helps provide the cloud cover and climate patterns that enable life to exist.

73 Making It to the Moon

Our moon is not the only moon in the solar system. Some other planets have moons also. Saturn has 10 moons! Our moon is Earth's closest neighbor in the solar system. Sometimes our moon is 225,727 miles away. Other times, it is 252,002 miles away. Why? Because the Moon revolves around Earth. It does not go around Earth in a perfect circle. So, sometimes its path takes it further away from our planet.

When our astronauts visited the Moon, they found dusty plains, high mountains and huge craters. There is no air or water on the Moon. That is why life cannot exist there. The astronauts had to wear space suits to protect their skin from the bright Sun. They had to take their own air to breathe. They had to take their own food and water.

Directions: Answer these questions about the Moon.

1. Circle the main idea:
   (The Moon travels around Earth, and the astronauts visited the Moon.)
   Astronauts found that the Moon—Earth's closest neighbor—has no air or water and cannot support life.

2. Write three things our astronauts found on the Moon.
   1) dusty plains 2) high mountains 3) huge craters

3. Make a list of what to take on a trip to the Moon.
   Answers will vary but can include: space suits, food, water and air

74 Bag of Bones

Are you scared of skeletons? You shouldn't be. There is a skeleton inside of you! The skeleton is made up of all the bones in your body. These 206 bones give you your shape. They also protect your heart and everything else inside. Your bones come in many sizes. Some are short. Some are long. Some are rounded. Some are very tiny. The outside of your bones looks solid. Inside, they are filled with a soft material called marrow. This is what keeps your bones alive. Red blood cells and most white blood cells are made here. These cells help feed the body and fight disease.

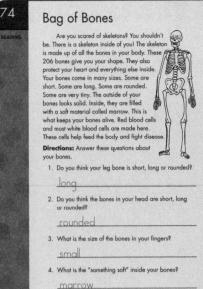

Directions: Answer these questions about your bones.

1. Do you think your leg bone is short, long or rounded?

   long

2. Do you think the bones in your head are short, long or rounded?

   rounded

3. What is the size of the bones in your fingers?

   small

4. What is the "something soft" inside your bones?

   marrow

75 Making Muscles

Can you make a fist? You could not do this without muscles. You need muscles to make your body move. You have muscles everywhere. There are muscles in your legs. There are even muscles in your tongue!

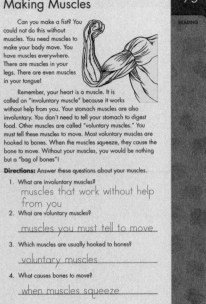

Remember, your heart is a muscle. It is called an "involuntary muscle" because it works without help from you. Your stomach muscles are also involuntary. You don't need to tell your stomach to digest food. Other muscles are called "voluntary muscles." You must tell these muscles to move. Most voluntary muscles are hooked to bones. When the muscles squeeze, they cause the bone to move. Without your muscles, you would be nothing but a "bag of bones"!

Directions: Answer these questions about your muscles.

1. What are involuntary muscles?

   muscles that work without help from you

2. What are voluntary muscles?

   muscles you must tell to move

3. Which muscles are usually hooked to bones?

   voluntary muscles

4. What causes bones to move?

   when muscles squeeze

76 Get a Clue!

Drawing a conclusion means to use clues to make a final decision about something. To draw a conclusion, you must read carefully.

Directions: Read each story carefully. Use the clues given to draw a conclusion about the story.

The boy and girl took turns pushing the shopping cart. They went up and down the aisles. Each time they stopped the cart, they would look at things on the shelf and decide what they needed. Jody asked her older brother, "Will I need a box of 48 crayons in Mrs. Charles' class?"

"Yes, I think so," he answered. Then, he turned to their mother and said, "I need some new notebooks. Can I get some?"

1. Where are they? _____ at the store
2. What are they doing buying school supplies
3. How do you know? Write at least two clue words that

   Mrs. Charles's class, notebooks, box of 48 crayons

Eric and Randy held on tight. They looked around them and saw that they were not the only ones holding on. The car moved slowly upward. As they turned and looked over the side, they noticed that the people far below them seemed to be getting smaller and smaller. "Hey, Eric, did I tell you this is my first time on one of these?" asked Randy. As they started down the hill at a frightening speed, Randy screamed, "And it may be my last!"

1. Where are they? _on a roller coaster_
2. How do you know? Write at least two clue words that

   car moved slowly upward, down at frightening speed

77 Mrs. Posy's Roses

Directions: Read the story. Then, answer the questions.

Mrs. Posy plants roses everywhere. She plants yellow roses near her front porch. She plants red roses near the back door. There are also pink roses and white roses in her yard. Every time the postal carrier comes to her house, he sneezes. "You should not plant so many flowers," he tells Mrs. Posy. Mrs. Posy just smiles.

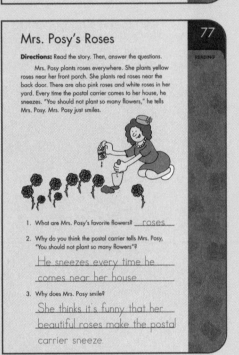

1. What are Mrs. Posy's favorite flowers? _roses_

2. Why do you think the postal carrier tells Mrs. Posy, "You should not plant so many flowers"?

   He sneezes every time he comes near her house.

3. Why does Mrs. Posy smile?

   She thinks it's funny that her beautiful roses make the postal carrier sneeze.

78 What's Hiding?

Directions: Read about caterpillars. Then, answer the questions.

Some people do not like caterpillars. Caterpillars look like fuzzy worms. They have many legs and they creep and crawl on trees and leaves. But a caterpillar is really the beginning of something else. After the caterpillar is very large, it spins a cocoon. It stays inside the cocoon for a few months. When the cocoon opens, something else is inside. It is very beautiful. It flies away.

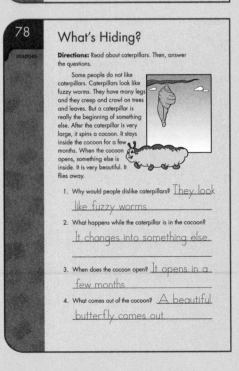

1. Why would people dislike caterpillars? They look like fuzzy worms

2. What happens while the caterpillar is in the cocoon?

   It changes into something else.

3. When does the cocoon open? It opens in a few months

4. What comes out of the cocoon? A beautiful butterfly comes out.

80 Egg-cellent!

Directions: Alphabetical order is putting words in the order in which they appear in the alphabet. Put the eggs in alphabetical order. The first and last words are done for you.

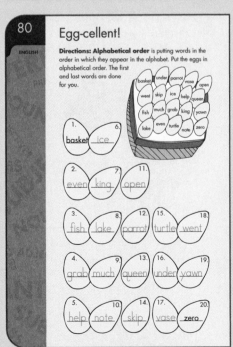

1. basket
6. ice

2. even
7. king
11. open

3. fish
8. lake
12. parrot
15. turtle
18. went

4. grab
13. much
16. queen
under
19. yawn

5. help
10. note
14. skip
17. vase
20. zero

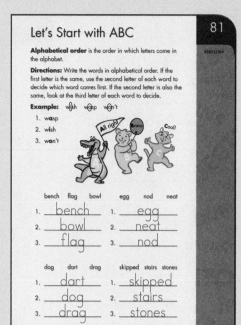

Let's Start with ABC

Alphabetical order is the order in which letters come in the alphabet.

Directions: Write the words in alphabetical order. If the first letter is the same, use the second letter of each word to decide which word comes first. If the second letter is also the same, look at the third letter of each word to decide.

Example: wish wasp won't
1. wasp
2. wish
3. won't

bench flag bowl   egg nod neat

1. bench   1. egg
2. bowl   2. neat
3. flag   3. nod

dog dart drag   skipped stairs stones

1. dart   1. skipped
2. dog   2. stairs
3. drag   3. stones

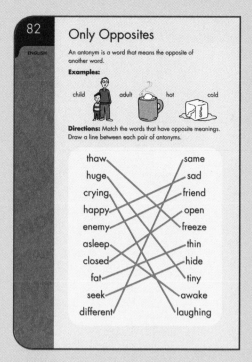

Only Opposites

An antonym is a word that means the opposite of another word.

Examples:

child   adult   hot   cold

Directions: Match the words that have opposite meanings. Draw a line between each pair of antonyms.

thaw — freeze
huge — tiny
crying — laughing
happy — sad
enemy — friend
asleep — awake
closed — open
fat — thin
seek — hide
different — same

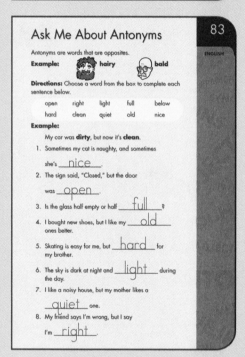

Ask Me About Antonyms

Antonyms are words that are opposites.

Example: hairy   bald

Directions: Choose a word from the box to complete each sentence below.

open   right   light   full   below
hard   clean   quiet   old   nice

Example:
My car was **dirty**, but now it's **clean**.

1. Sometimes my cat is naughty, and sometimes she's nice.
2. The sign said, "Closed," but the door was open.
3. Is the glass half empty or half full?
4. I bought new shoes, but I like my old ones better.
5. Skating is easy for me, but hard for my brother.
6. The sky is dark at night and light during the day.
7. I like a noisy house, but my mother likes a quiet one.
8. My friend says I'm wrong, but I say I'm right.

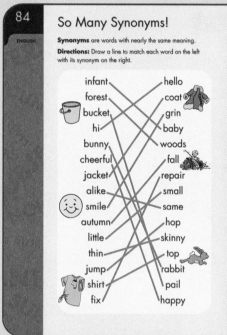

So Many Synonyms!

Synonyms are words with nearly the same meaning.

Directions: Draw a line to match each word on the left with its synonym on the right.

infant — baby
forest — woods
bucket — pail
hi — hello
bunny — rabbit
cheerful — happy
jacket — coat
alike — same
smile — grin
autumn — fall
little — small
thin — skinny
jump — hop
shirt — top
fix — repair

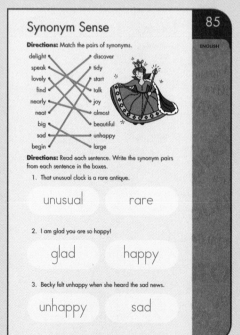

Synonym Sense

Directions: Match the pairs of synonyms.

delight — joy
speak — talk
lovely — beautiful
find — discover
nearly — almost
neat — tidy
big — large
sad — unhappy
begin — start

Directions: Read each sentence. Write the synonym pairs from each sentence in the boxes.

1. That unusual clock is a rare antique.

unusual   rare

2. I am glad you are so happy!

glad   happy

3. Becky felt unhappy when she heard the sad news.

unhappy   sad

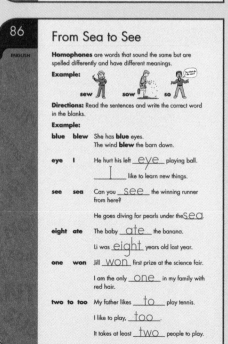

From Sea to See

Homophones are words that sound the same but are spelled differently and have different meanings.

Example:

sew   sow   so

Directions: Read the sentences and write the correct word in the blanks.

Example:

blue   blew   She has **blue** eyes.
The wind **blew** the barn down.

eye   I   He hurt his left eye playing ball.
I like to learn new things.

see   sea   Can you see the winning runner from here?
He goes diving for pearls under the sea.

eight   ate   The baby ate the banana.
Li was eight years old last year.

one   won   Jill won first prize at the science fair.
I am the only one in my family with red hair.

two   to   too   My father likes to play tennis.
I like to play, too.
It takes at least two people to play.

Hooray for Homophones

87 ENGLISH

Homophones are words that sound the same but have different spellings and meanings.

Directions: Complete each sentence using a word from the box.

| blew | night | blue | knight | hour | in |
| ant | inn | our | aunt | meet | meat |

1. A red __ant__ crawled up the wall.
2. It will be one __hour__ before we can go back home.
3. Will you __meet__ us later?
4. We plan to stay at an __inn__ during our trip.
5. The king had a __knight__ who fought bravely.
6. The wind __blew__ so hard that I almost lost my hat.
7. His jacket was __blue__.
8. My __aunt__ plans to visit us this week.
9. I will come __in__ when it gets too cold outside.
10. It was late at __night__ when we finally got there.
11. Do you eat red __meat__?
12. Come over to see __our__ new cat.

Know Your Nouns

88 ENGLISH

Common nouns are nouns that name any member of a group of people, places or things, rather than specific people, places or things.

Directions: Read the sentences below and write the common noun found in each sentence.

Example: __socks__ My socks do not match.

1. __bird__ The bird could not fly.
2. __jelly beans__ Ben likes to eat jelly beans.
3. __mother__ I am going to meet my mother.
4. __lake__ We will go swimming in the lake tomorrow.
5. __flowers__ I hope the flowers will grow quickly.
6. __eggs__ We colored eggs together.
7. __bicycle__ It is easy to ride a bicycle.
8. __cousin__ My cousin is very tall.
9. __boat__ Ted and Aliyah went fishing in their boat.
10. __prize__ They won a prize yesterday.
11. __ankle__ She fell down and twisted her ankle.
12. __brother__ My brother was born today.

Naming Nouns

89 ENGLISH

Proper nouns are names of specific people, places or things. Proper nouns begin with a capital letter.

Directions: Read the sentences below and circle the proper nouns found in each sentence.

Example: (Aunt Frances) gave me a puppy for my birthday.

1. We lived on (Jackson Street) before we moved to our new house.
2. (Angela's) birthday party is tomorrow night.
3. We drove through (Cheyenne, Wyoming) on our way home.
4. (Dr. Charles) always gives me a treat for not crying.
5. (George Washington) was our first president.
6. Our class took a field trip to the (Johnson Flower Farm.)
7. (Uncle Jack) lives in (New York City.)
8. (Jada) and (Elizabeth) are best friends.
9. We buy doughnuts at the (Grayson Bakery.)
10. My favorite movie is (E.T.)
11. We flew to (Miami, Florida) in a plane.
12. We go to (Riverfront Stadium) to watch the baseball games.

Plenty of Plurals

90 ENGLISH

A **plural** is more than one person, place or thing. We usually add an **s** to show that a noun names more than one. If a noun ends in **x**, **ch**, **sh** or **s**, we add **es** to the word.

Example: pizza → pizzas

Directions: Write the plural of the words below.

Example: dog + s = dogs

Example: peach + es = peaches

cat	__cats__	lunch	__lunches__
boot	__boots__	bunch	__bunches__
house	__houses__	punch	__punches__

Example: ax + es = axes

Example: glass + es = glasses

fox	__foxes__	mess	__messes__
tax	__taxes__	guess	__guesses__
box	__boxes__	class	__classes__

Example: dish + es = dishes

bush	__bushes__	walrus	
ash	__ashes__		
brush	__brushes__	walruses	

Plenty of Plurals

91 ENGLISH

To write the plural forms of words ending in **y**, we change the **y** to **ie** and add **s**.

Example: pony __ponies__

Directions: Write the plural of each noun on the lines below.

berry	__berries__
cherry	__cherries__
bunny	__bunnies__
penny	__pennies__
family	__families__
candy	__candies__
party	__parties__

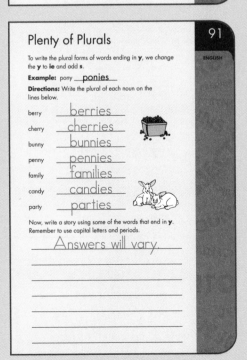

Now, write a story using some of the words that end in **y**. Remember to use capital letters and periods.

__Answers will vary.__

Under the Big Top

92 ENGLISH

Possessive nouns tell who or what is the owner of something. With singular nouns, we use an apostrophe **before** the **s**. With plural nouns, we use an apostrophe **after** the **s**.

Example:

singular: one elephant
The **elephant's** dance was wonderful.

plural: more than one elephant
The **elephants'** dance was wonderful.

Directions: Put the apostrophe in the correct place in each bold word. Then, write the word in the blank.

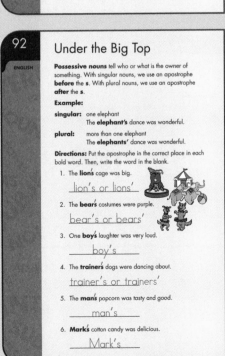

1. The **lions** cage was big.
__lion's or lions'__
2. The **bears** costumes were purple.
__bear's or bears'__
3. One **boys** laughter was very loud.
__boy's__
4. The **trainers** dogs were dancing about.
__trainer's or trainers'__
5. The **mans** popcorn was tasty and good.
__man's__
6. **Marks** cotton candy was delicious.
__Mark's__

238

That's Mine!   93

Directions: Circle the correct possessive noun in each sentence and write it in the blank.

Example: One ___girl's___ mother is a teacher.
(girl's)   girls'

1. The ___cat's___ tail is long.
(cat's)   cats'

2. One ___boy's___ baseball bat is aluminum.
(boy's)   boys'

3. Both ___waitresses'___ aprons are white.
(waitresses')   waitress's

4. My ___grandmother'___s apple pie is the best!
(grandmother's)   grandmothers'

5. My five ___brothers'___ uniforms are dirty.
brother's   (brothers')

6. The ___child's___ doll is pretty.
(child's)   childs'

Pronoun Power!   94

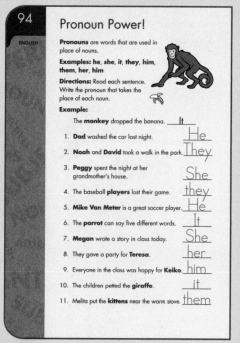

Pronouns are words that are used in place of nouns.

Examples: he, she, it, they, him, them, her, him

Directions: Read each sentence. Write the pronoun that takes the place of each noun.

Example:
The **monkey** dropped the banana. ___It___

1. **Dad** washed the car last night. ___He___
2. **Noah** and **David** took a walk in the park. ___They___
3. **Peggy** spent the night at her grandmother's house. ___She___
4. The baseball **players** lost their game. ___they___
5. **Mike Van Meter** is a great soccer player. ___He___
6. The **parrot** can say five different words. ___It___
7. **Megan** wrote a story in class today. ___She___
8. They gave a party for **Teresa**. ___her___
9. Everyone in the class was happy for **Keiko**. ___him___
10. The children petted the **giraffe**. ___it___
11. Melita put the **kittens** near the warm stove. ___them___

Getting Possessive   95

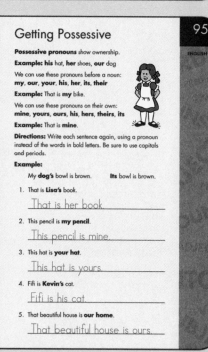

Possessive pronouns show ownership.
Example: his hat, **her** shoes, **our** dog

We can use these pronouns before a noun:
my, our, your, his, her, its, their
Example: That is **my** bike.

We can use these pronouns on their own:
mine, yours, ours, his, hers, theirs, its
Example: That is **mine**.

Directions: Write each sentence again, using a pronoun instead of the words in bold letters. Be sure to use capitals and periods.

Example:
My **dog's** bowl is brown.   **Its** bowl is brown.

1. That is **Lisa's** book.
   That is her book.

2. This pencil is **my pencil.**
   This pencil is mine.

3. This hat is **your hat.**
   This hat is yours.

4. Fifi is **Kevin's** cat.
   Fifi is his cat.

5. That beautiful house is **our home**.
   That beautiful house is ours.

Wild for Pets   96

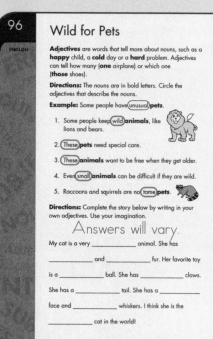

Adjectives are words that tell more about nouns, such as a **happy** child, a **cold** day or a **hard** problem. Adjectives can tell how many (**one** airplane) or which one (**those** shoes).

Directions: The nouns are in bold letters. Circle the adjectives that describe the nouns.

Example: Some people have (unusual) **pets**.

1. Some people keep (wild) **animals**, like lions and bears.
2. (These) **pets** need special care.
3. (These) **animals** want to be free when they get older.
4. Even (small) **animals** can be difficult if they are wild.
5. Raccoons and squirrels are no (tame) **pets**.

Directions: Complete the story below by writing in your own adjectives. Use your imagination.

Answers will vary.

My cat is a very _____ animal. She has _____ and _____ fur. Her favorite toy is a _____ ball. She has _____ claws. She has a _____ tail. She has a _____ face and _____ whiskers. I think she is the _____ cat in the world!

Tell Me More!   97

Directions: Underline the nouns in each sentence below. Then, draw an arrow from each adjective to the noun it describes.

Example:
A playpus is a funny animal that lives in Australia.

1. This animal likes to swim.
2. The nose looks like a duck's bill.
3. It has a broad tail like a beaver.
4. Platypuses are great swimmers.
5. They have webbed feet which help them swim.
6. Their flat tails also help them move through the water.
7. The platypus is an unusual mammal because it lays eggs.
8. The eggs look like reptile eggs.
9. Platypuses can lay three eggs at a time.

Prefix Pros   98

Prefixes are special word parts added to the beginnings of words. Prefixes change the meaning of words.

Prefix	Meaning	Example
un	not	**un**happy
re	again	**re**do
pre	before	**pre**view
mis	wrong	**mis**understanding
dis	opposite	**dis**obey

Directions: Circle the word that begins with a prefix. Then, write the prefix and the root word.

1. The dog was (unfriendly).
   un + friendly
2. The movie (preview) was interesting.
   pre + view
3. The referee called an (unfair) penalty.
   un + fair
4. Please do not (misbehave).
   mis + behave
5. My parents (disapprove) of that show.
   dis + approve
6. I had to (redo) the assignment.
   re + do

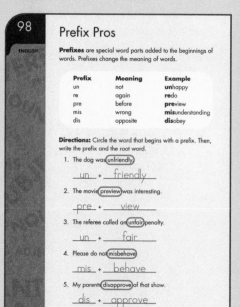

Super Suffixes

99
ENGLISH

Suffixes are word parts added to the ends of words. Suffixes change the meaning of words.

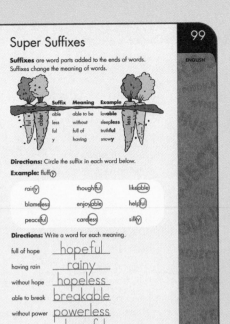

Suffix	Meaning	Example
able	able to be	lov**able**
less	without	sleep**less**
ful	full of	truth**ful**
y	having	snow**y**

Directions: Circle the suffix in each word below.

Example: fluff(y)

rain(y)   though(ful)   like(able)

blame(less)   enjoy(able)   help(ful)

peace(ful)   care(less)   sill(y)

Directions: Write a word for each meaning.

full of hope	hopeful
having rain	rainy
without hope	hopeless
able to break	breakable
without power	powerless
full of cheer	cheerful

Web Weavers

100
ENGLISH

A **verb** in a sentence is usually an action word, a word that tells what someone or something does. **Examples: run, jump, skip.**

Directions: Draw a box around the verb in each sentence below.

1. Spiders spin webs of silk.

2. A spider waits in the center of the web for its meals.

3. A spider sinks its sharp fangs into insects.

4. Spiders eat many insects.

5. Spiders make their nests with silk.

Directions: Choose the correct verb from the box and write it in the sentences below.

hides   swims   eat   grabs

1. A crab spider __hides__ deep inside a flower where it cannot be seen.

2. The crab spider __grabs__ insects when they land on the flower.

3. The wolf spider is good because it __eats__ wasps.

4. The water spider __swims__ under water.

Action All Around

101
ENGLISH

When a verb tells what one person or thing is doing now, it usually ends in **s. Example:** She **sings.**

When a verb is used with **you, I** or **we**, we do not add an **s.**

Example: I sing.

Directions: Write the correct verb in each sentence.

I __write__ a newspaper about our street.
writes   write

1. My sister __helps__ me sometimes.
helps   help

2. She __draws__ the pictures.
draw   draws

3. We __deliver__ them together.
delivers   deliver

4. I __tell__ the news about all the people.
tell   tells

5. Mr. Macon __grows__ the most beautiful flowers.
grow   grows

6. Mrs. Cohen __talks__ to her plants.
talks   talk

7. Kevin Turner __lets__ his dog loose everyday.
lets   let

9. You must __think__ I live on an interesting street.
thinks   think

Happy to Help

102
ENGLISH

A **helping verb** is a verb that goes along with another verb.

Examples: might, shall and **are**

Directions: Write a helping verb from the box with each action verb.

can	could	must	might may
would	should	will	shall did
does	do	had	have has
am	are	were	is
be	being	been	

Answers will vary but may include:

1. Mom __may__ buy my new soccer shoes tonight.

2. Yesterday, my old soccer shoes __were__ ripped by the cat.

3. I __am__ going to ask my brother to go to the game.

4. He usually __does__ not like soccer.

5. But, he __will__ go with me because I am his sister.

6. He __has__ promised to watch the entire soccer game.

7. He has __been__ helping me with my homework.

8. I __can__ spell a lot better because of his help.

It's All in the Past

103
ENGLISH

The **past tense** of a verb tells about something that has already happened. We add a **d** or an **ed** to most verbs to show that something has already happened.

Directions: Use the verb from the first sentence to complete the second sentence.

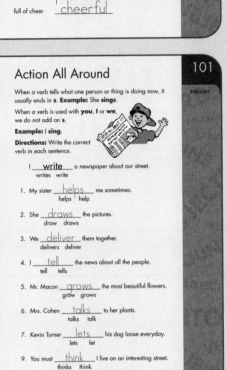

Example:

Please **walk** the dog.   I already __walked__ her.

1. The flowers look good.   They __looked__ better yesterday.

2. Please accept my gift.   I __accepted__ it for my sister.

3. I wonder who will win.   I __wondered__ about it all night.

4. He will saw the wood.   He __sawed__ some last week.

5. Fold the paper neatly.   She __folded__ her paper.

6. Let's cook outside tonight.   We __cooked__ outside last night.

7. Do not block the way.   They __blocked__ the entire street.

8. Follow my car.   We __followed__ them down the street.

No Time Like the Present

104
ENGLISH

The **present tense** of a verb tells about something that is happening now, happens often or is about to happen. These verbs can be written two ways: The bird sings. The bird is sing**ing.**

Directions: Write each sentence again, using the verb **is** and writing the **ing** form of the verb.

Example:

He cooks the cheeseburgers.

__He is cooking the cheeseburgers.__

1. Sharon dances to that song.

__Sharon is dancing to that song.__

2. Frank washed the car.

__Frank is washing the car.__

3. Mr. Benson smiles at me.

__Mr. Benson is smiling at me.__

Write a verb for the sentences below that tells something that is happening now. Be sure to use the verb **is** and the **ing** form of the verb.

Example: Answers will vary.

The big, brown dog __is barking__

1. The little baby _____

2. Most nine-year-olds _____

3. The monster on television _____

Seeing the Future

105

ENGLISH

The **future tense** of a verb tells about something that has not happened yet but will happen in the future. **Will** or **shall** is usually used with future tense.

Directions: Change the verb tense in each sentence to future tense.

Example:

She cooks dinner.

She will cook dinner.

1. He plays baseball.

   He will play baseball.

2. She walks to school.

   She will walk to school.

3. Samir talks to the teacher.

   Samir will talk to the teacher.

4. I remember to vote.

   I will remember to vote.

5. Jack mows the lawn every week.

   Jack will mow the lawn every week.

Out of the Ordinary

106

ENGLISH

Irregular verbs are verbs that do not change from the present tense to the past tense in the regular way with **d** or **ed**.

Example: sing, **sang**

Directions: Read the sentence and underline the verbs. Choose the past-tense form from the box and write it next to the sentence.

blow — blew	fly — flew
come — came	give — gave
take — took	wear — wore
make — made	grow — grew

Example:

Dad will <u>make</u> a cake tonight.   _made_

1. I will probably <u>grow</u> another inch this year.   _grew_
2. I will <u>blow</u> out the candles.   _blew_
3. Everyone will <u>give</u> me presents.   _gave_
4. I will <u>wear</u> my favorite red shirt.   _wore_
5. My cousins will <u>come</u> from out of town.   _came_
6. It will <u>take</u> them four hours.   _took_
7. My Aunt Betty will <u>fly</u> in from Cleveland.   _flew_

Breaking the Rules

107

ENGLISH

Directions: Circle the verb that completes each sentence.

1. Scientists will try to (find) found) the cure.

2. Eric (brings, (brought)) his lunch to school yesterday.

3. Everyday, Betsy ((sings) sang) all the way home.

4. Tomas (breaks, (broke)) the vase last night.

5. The ice had (freezes, (frozen)) in the tray.

6. Mitzi has (swims, (swum)) in that pool before.

7. Now I ((choose) chose) to exercise daily.

8. The teacher has (rings, (rung)) the bell.

To Be or Not to Be

108

ENGLISH

The verb **be** is different from all other verbs. The present-tense forms of **be** are **am**, **is** and **are**. The past-tense forms of **be** are **was** and **were**. The verb **to be** is written in the following ways:

singular: I am, you are, he is, she is, it is

plural: we are, you are, they are

Directions: Choose the correct form of be from the words in the box and write it in each sentence.

are	am	is	was	were

Example:

I _am_ feeling good at this moment.

1. My sister _is_ a good singer.
2. You _are_ going to the store with me.
3. Emma _was_ at the movies last week.
4. Marcos and Tom _are_ best friends.
5. He _is_ happy about the surprise.
6. The cat _is_ hungry.
7. I _am_ going to the ball game.

Think of a Link

109

ENGLISH

Linking verbs connect the noun to a descriptive word. Linking verbs are often forms of the verb **be**.

Directions: The linking verb is underlined in each sentence. Circle the two words that are being connected.

Example: The (cat) is (fat)

1. My favorite (food) is (pizza)

2. The (car) was (red.)

3. (I) am (tired)

4. (Books) are (fun)

5. (Pears) taste (juicy)

6. The (airplane) looks (large)

Adverb Alert

110

ENGLISH

Adverbs are words that usually describe verbs. They tell where, how or when.

Directions: Circle the adverb in each of the following sentences.

Example: The doctor worked (carefully)

1. The skater moved (gracefully) across the ice.

2. Their call was returned (quickly)

3. We (easily) learned the new words.

4. He did the work (perfectly)

Directions: Complete the sentences below by writing your own adverbs in the blanks.

Answers will vary.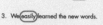

1. The dog barked _____
2. The baby smiled _____
3. She wrote her name _____

111 ENGLISH — Adverb Attitude

Directions: Read each sentence. Then, answer the questions on the lines below.

Example:

Charles ate hungrily.   **who?** Charles

what? ate   **how?** hungrily

1. She dances slowly.   **who?** She

   what? dances   **how?** slowly

2. The girl spoke carefully.   **who?** girl

   what? spoke   **how?** carefully

3. My brother ran quickly.   **who?** brother

   what? ran   **how?** quickly

4. Olivia walks home often.   **who?** Olivia

   what? walks   **how?** often

112 ENGLISH — Preposition Prep

Prepositions show relationships between a noun or pronoun and another word in the sentence. The preposition comes before that noun or pronoun.

Example: The book is (on) the table.

Common Prepositions

above	behind	by	near	over
across	below	in	off	through
around	beside	inside	on	under

Directions: Circle the prepositions in each sentence.

1. The dog ran fast (around) the house.

2. The plates (in) the cupboard were clean.

3. Put the card (inside) the envelope.

4. The towel (on) the sink was wet.

5. I planted flowers (in) my garden.

6. My kite flew high (above) the trees.

7. The chair (near) the counter was sticky.

8. (Under) the ground, worms lived in their homes.

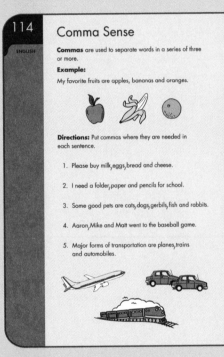

113 ENGLISH — A Is for Article

Articles are words used before nouns. **A**, **an** and **the** are articles. We use **a** before words that begin with a consonant. We use **an** before words that begin with a vowel.

Example: a peach   an apple

Directions: Write **a** or **an** in the sentences below.

Example:

My bike had **a** flat tire.

1. They brought **a** goat to the farm.

2. My mom wears **an** old pair of shoes to mow the lawn.

3. We had **a** party for my grandfather.

4. Everybody had **an** ice-cream cone after the game.

5. We bought **a** picnic table for our backyard.

6. We saw **a** lion sleeping in the shade.

7. It was **an** evening to be remembered.

8. He brought **a** blanket to the game.

9. **An** exit sign was above the door.

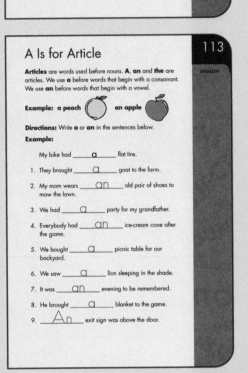

114 ENGLISH — Comma Sense

Commas are used to separate words in a series of three or more.

Example:

My favorite fruits are apples, bananas and oranges.

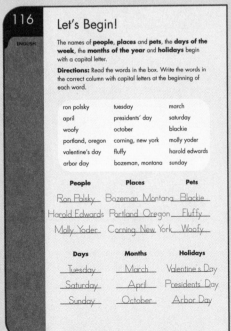

Directions: Put commas where they are needed in each sentence.

1. Please buy milk, eggs, bread and cheese.

2. I need a folder, paper and pencils for school.

3. Some good pets are cats, dogs, gerbils, fish and rabbits.

4. Aaron, Mike and Matt went to the baseball game.

5. Major forms of transportation are planes, trains and automobiles.

115 ENGLISH — Counting on Commas

We use commas to separate the day from the year.

Example: May 13, 1950

Directions: Write the dates in the blanks. Put the commas in and capitalize the name of each month.

Example:

Jack and Dave were born on february 22 1982

February 22, 1982

1. My father's birthday is may 19 1948.

   May 19, 1948

2. My sister was fourteen on december 13 1994.

   December 13, 1994

3. Sonya's seventh birthday was on november 30 1998.

   November 30, 1998

4. october 13 2009 was the last day I saw my lost cat.

   October 13, 2009

5. On april 17 1997, we saw the Grand Canyon.

   April 17, 1997

6. Our vacation lasted from april 2 2007 to april 26 2007.

   April 2, 2007

   April 26, 2007

116 ENGLISH — Let's Begin!

The names of **people**, **places** and **pets**, the **days of the week**, the **months of the year** and **holidays** begin with a capital letter.

Directions: Read the words in the box. Write the words in the correct column with capital letters at the beginning of each word.

ron polsky	tuesday	march
april	presidents' day	saturday
woofy	october	blackie
portland, oregon	corning, new york	molly yoder
valentine's day	fluffy	harold edwards
arbor day	bozeman, montana	sunday

People	Places	Pets
Ron Polsky	Bozeman, Montana	Blackie
Harold Edwards	Portland, Oregon	Fluffy
Molly Yoder	Corning, New York	Woofy

Days	Months	Holidays
Tuesday	March	Valentine's Day
Saturday	April	Presidents' Day
Sunday	October	Arbor Day

Know Your Place

117

ENGLISH

We capitalize the names of cities and states. We use a comma to separate the name of a city and a state.

Directions: Use capital letters and commas to write the names of the cities and states correctly.

Example:

sioux falls south dakota

Sioux Falls, South Dakota

1. plymouth massachusettes

Plymouth, Massachusettes

2. boston massachusettes

Boston, Massachusettes

3. philadelphia pennsylvania

Philadelphia, Pennsylvania

4. white plains new york

White Plains, New York

5. newport rhode island

Newport, Rhode Island

6. yorktown virginia

Yorktown, Virginia

Label It!

118

ENGLISH

Nouns, pronouns, verbs, adjectives, adverbs and prepositions are all **parts of speech**.

Directions: Label the words in each sentence with the correct part of speech.

Example: The cat is fat.
article / noun / verb / adjective

1. My cow walks in the barn.
pronoun / noun / verb / preposition / article / noun

2. Red flowers grow in the garden.
adjective / noun / verb / preposition / article / noun

3. The large dog was excited.
article / adjective / noun / verb / adjective

Fill in a Story

119

ENGLISH

Directions: Ask someone to give you nouns, verbs, adjectives and pronouns where shown. Write them in the blanks. Read the story to your friend when you finish.

Answers will vary.

I went for a _____. I found a really
(noun)

big _____. It was so _____ that
(noun)   (adjective)

I _____ all the way home. I put it in
(verb)

my _____. To my amazement, it began
(noun)

to _____. I _____. I took it to
(verb)   (past-tense verb)

my _____. I showed it to all my _____.
(place)   (plural noun)

I decided to _____ it in a box and wrap it up
(verb)

with _____ paper. I gave it to _____
(adjective)   (person)

for a present. When _____ opened it, _____
(pronoun)   (pronoun)

_____, _____ shouted, "Thank you!
(past-tense verb)   (pronoun)

This is the best _____ I've ever had!"
(noun)

Zany Zebras

120

ENGLISH

A **subject** tells who or what the sentence is about.

Directions: Underline the subject in the following sentences.

Example:

The zebra is a large animal.

1. Zebras live in Africa.

2. Zebras are related to horses.

3. Horses have longer hair than zebras.

4. Zebras are good runners.

5. Their feet are protected by their hooves.

6. Some animals live in groups.

7. These groups are called herds.

8. Zebras live in herds with other grazing animals.

9. Grazing animals eat mostly grass.

Twice as Nice

121

ENGLISH

Compound subjects are two or more nouns that have the same predicate.

Directions: Combine the subjects to create one sentence with a compound subject.

Example: Jill can swing.
Whitney can swing.
Luke can swing.
Jill, Whitney and Luke can swing.

1. Roses grow in the garden. Tulips grow in the garden.

Roses and tulips grow in the garden.

2. Apples are fruit. Oranges are fruit. Bananas are fruit.

Apples, oranges and bananas are fruit.

3. Bears live in the zoo. Monkeys live in the zoo.

Bears and monkeys live in the zoo.

4. Jackets keep us warm. Sweaters keep us warm.

Jackets and sweaters keep us warm.

Woodpecking Wonders

122

ENGLISH

A **predicate** usually tells what the subject is doing, has done, or will do.

Directions: Underline the predicate in the following sentences.

Example: Woodpeckers live in trees.

1. They hunt for insects in the trees.

2. Woodpeckers have strong beaks.

3. They can peck through the bark.

4. The pecking sound can be heard from far away.

Directions: Circle the groups of words that can be predicates.

(have long tongues)   (pick up insects)

hole in bark   sticky substance

(help it to climb trees)   tree bark

Now, choose the correct predicates from above to finish these sentences.

1. Woodpeckers have long tongues

2. They use their tongues to pick up insects

3. Its strong feet help it to climb trees

Double the Action

123

ENGLISH

Compound predicates have two or more verbs that have the same subject.

Directions: Combine the predicates to create one sentence with a compound predicate.

Example: We went to the zoo.
We watched the monkeys.
We went to the zoo and watched the monkeys.

1. Students read their books. Students do their work.

   <u>Students read their books and do their work.</u>

2. Dogs can bark loudly. Dogs can do tricks.

   <u>Dogs can bark loudly and do tricks.</u>

3. The football player caught the ball. The football player ran.

   <u>The football player caught the ball and ran.</u>

4. My dad sawed wood. My dad stacked wood.

   <u>My dad sawed and stacked wood</u>

5. My teddy bear sleeps with me. My teddy bear likes hugs.

   <u>My teddy bear sleeps with me and likes hugs.</u>

Prickly Porcupines

124

ENGLISH

Directions: Every sentence has two main parts—the subject and the predicate. Draw one line under the subject and two lines under the predicate in each sentence below.

Example:

<u>Porcupines</u> <u><u>are related to mice and rats.</u></u>

1. <u>They</u> <u><u>are large rodents.</u></u>

2. <u>Porcupines</u> <u><u>have long, sharp quills.</u></u>

3. <u>The quills</u> <u><u>stand up straight when it is angry.</u></u>

4. <u>Most animals</u> <u><u>stay away from porcupines.</u></u>

5. <u>Their quills</u> <u><u>hurt other animals.</u></u>

6. <u>Porcupines</u> <u><u>sleep under rocks or bushes.</u></u>

7. <u>They</u> <u><u>sleep during the day.</u></u>

8. <u>Porcupines</u> <u><u>eat plants at night.</u></u>

9. <u>North America</u> <u><u>has some porcupines.</u></u>

10. <u>They</u> <u><u>are called New World porcupines.</u></u>

11. <u>New World porcupines</u> <u><u>can climb trees.</u></u>

Putting It All Together

125

ENGLISH

Directions: Draw one line under the subjects and two lines under the predicates in the sentences below.

1. <u>My mom</u> <u><u>likes to plant flowers.</u></u>

2. <u>Our neighbors</u> <u><u>walk their dog.</u></u>

3. <u>Our car</u> <u><u>needs gas.</u></u>

4. <u>The children</u> <u><u>play house.</u></u>

5. <u>Movies and popcorn</u> <u><u>go well together.</u></u>

6. <u>Peanut butter and jelly</u> <u><u>is my favorite kind of sandwich.</u></u>

7. <u>Bill, Akiko and Brittany</u> <u><u>ride to the park.</u></u>

8. <u>We</u> <u><u>use pencils, markers and pens to write on paper.</u></u>

9. <u>Trees and shrubs</u> <u><u>need special care.</u></u>

Shark Attack!

126

ENGLISH

A **sentence** tells a complete idea.

Directions: Circle the groups of words that tell a complete idea.

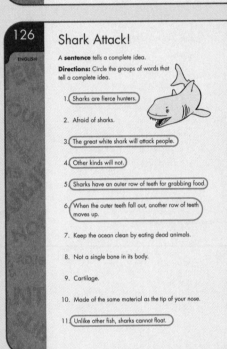

1. (Sharks are fierce hunters.)

2. Afraid of sharks.

3. (The great white shark will attack people.)

4. (Other kinds will not.)

5. (Sharks have an outer row of teeth for grabbing food.)

6. (When the outer teeth fall out, another row of teeth moves up.)

7. Keep the ocean clean by eating dead animals.

8. Not a single bone in its body.

9. Cartilage.

10. Made of the same material as the tip of your nose.

11. (Unlike other fish, sharks cannot float.)

Downtown Discoveries

127

ENGLISH

Directions: Complete the story, using sentences that tell complete ideas.

<u>Answers will vary.</u>

trip downtown. I was so excited I _____

At the bus stop, we saw _____. Our bus driver

_____

When we got off the bus _____

_____. I'd never seen so many

_____.

My favorite part was when we _____

We stopped to eat _____

_____

_____. I bought a _____

_____

When we got home, I told my friend, " _____

_____ "

Wondering About Walruses

128

ENGLISH

Statements are sentences that tell about something. Statements begin with a capital letter and end with a period.
Questions are sentences that ask about something. Questions begin with a capital letter and end with a question mark.

Directions: Rewrite the sentences using capital letters and either a period or a question mark.

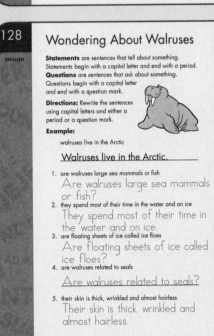

Example:

walruses live in the Arctic

<u>Walruses live in the Arctic.</u>

1. are walruses large sea mammals or fish

   <u>Are walruses large sea mammals or fish?</u>

2. they spend most of their time in the water and on ice

   <u>They spend most of their time in the water and on ice.</u>

3. are floating sheets of ice called ice floes

   <u>Are floating sheets of ice called ice floes?</u>

4. are walruses related to seals

   <u>Are walruses related to seals?</u>

5. their skin is thick, wrinkled and almost hairless

   <u>Their skin is thick, wrinkled and almost hairless.</u>

Snow Day! — 129
ENGLISH

Exclamation points are used for sentences that express strong feelings. These sentences can have one or two words or be very long.

Example: Wait! or **Don't forget to call!**

Directions: Add an exclamation point at the end of sentences that express strong feelings. Add a period at the end of the statements.

1. My parents and I were watching television.
2. The snow began falling around noon.
3. Wow!
4. The snow was really coming down!
5. We turned the television off and looked out the window.
6. The snow looked like a white blanket.
7. How beautiful!
8. We decided to put on our coats and go outside.
9. Hurry!
10. Get your sled.
11. All the people on the street came out to see the snow.
12. How wonderful!

Contraction Action — 130
ENGLISH

Contractions are shortened forms of two words. We use apostrophes to show where letters are missing.

Example: It is = it's

Directions: Write the words that are used in each contraction.

we're __we__ + __are__   they'll __they__ + __will__
you'll __you__ + __will__   aren't __are__ + __not__
I'm __I__ + __am__   isn't __is__ + __not__

Directions: Write the contraction for the two words shown.

you have __you've__
have not __haven't__
had not __hadn't__
we will __we'll__
they are __they're__
he is __he's__
she had __she'd__
it will __it'll__

Make Your Mark — 131
ENGLISH

Apostrophes are used to show ownership by placing an **s** at the end of a single person, place or thing.

Example: Mary**'s** cat

Directions: Write the apostrophes in the contractions below.

Example: We shouldn**'**t be going to their house so late at night.

1. We didn't think that the ice cream would melt so fast.
2. They're never around when we're ready to go.
3. Didn't you need to make a phone call?

Directions: Add an apostrophe and an **s** to the words to show ownership of a person, place or thing.

Example: Jill**'s** bike is broken.

1. That is Holly's flower garden.
2. Ivan's new skates are black and green.
3. Mom threw away Dad's old shoes.

You Said It! — 132
ENGLISH

Quotation marks are punctuation marks that tell what is said by a person. Quotation marks go before the first word and after the punctuation of a direct quote. The first word of a direct quote begins with a capital letter.

Example: Katie said, "Never go in the water without a friend."

Directions: Put quotation marks around the correct words in the sentences below.

Example: "Wait for me, please," said Paloma.

1. "John, would you like to visit a jungle?" asked his uncle.
2. The police officer said, "Don't worry, we'll help you."
3. James shouted, "Hit a home run!"
4. My friend Olivia said, "I really don't like cheeseburgers."

Directions: Write your own quotations by answering the questions below. Be sure to put quotation marks around your words.

1. What would you say if you saw a dinosaur?

   Answers will vary.

2. What would your best friend say if your hair turned purple?

   Answers will vary.

Taking a Ride — 133
ENGLISH

Directions: Put quotation marks around the correct words in the sentences below.

1. Can we go for a bike ride? asked Katrina.
   "Can we go for a bike ride?" asked Katrina.

2. Yes, said Mom.
   "Yes," said Mom.

3. Let's go to the park, said Mike.
   "Let's go to the park," said Mike.

4. Great idea! said Mom.
   "Great idea!" said Mom.

5. How long until we get there? asked Katrina.
   "How long until we get there?" asked Katrina.

6. Soon, said Mike.
   "Soon," said Mike.

7. Here we are! exclaimed Mom.
   "Here we are!" exclaimed Mom.

What's It All About? — 134
ENGLISH

A **topic sentence** is usually the first sentence in a paragraph. It tells what the story will be about.

Directions: Read the following sentences. Circle the topic sentence that should go first in the paragraph that follows.

(Rainbows have seven colors.)

There's a pot of gold.

I like rainbows.

The colors are red, orange, yellow, green, blue, indigo and violet. Red forms the outer edge, with violet on the inside of the rainbow.

He cut down a cherry tree.

His wife was named Martha.

(George Washington was a good president.)

He helped our country get started. He chose intelligent leaders to help him run the country.

(Mark Twain was a great author.)

Mark Twain was unhappy sometimes.

Mark Twain was born in Missouri.

One of his most famous books is *Huckleberry Finn*. He wrote many other great books.

Middle Matters — 135

ENGLISH

Middle sentences support the topic sentence. They tell more about it.

Directions: Underline the middle sentences that support each topic sentence below.

Topic Sentence:
Penguins are birds that cannot fly.

Pelicans can spear fish with their sharp bills.
Many penguins waddle or hop about on land.
Even though they cannot fly, they are excellent swimmers.
Pelicans keep their food in a pouch.

Topic Sentence:
Volleyball is a team sport in which the players hit the ball over the net.

There are two teams with six players on each team.
My friend John would rather play tennis with Akiko.
Players can use their heads or their hands.
I broke my hand once playing handball.

Topic Sentence:
Pikes Peak is the most famous of all the Rocky Mountains.

Some mountains have more trees than other mountains.
Many people like to climb to the top.
Many people like to ski and camp there, too.
The weather is colder at the top of most mountains.

136 — Wrapping It Up

ENGLISH

Ending sentences are sentences that tie the story together.

Directions: Choose the correct ending sentence for each story from the sentences below. Write it at the end of the paragraph.

It was a new pair of shoes!
It was all the corn on the cob I could eat!
It was a new eraser!

Corn on the Cob

Corn on the cob used to be my favorite food. That is, until I lost my four front teeth. For one whole year, I had to sit and watch everyone else eat my favorite food without me. Mom gave me creamed corn, but it just wasn't the same. When my teeth finally came in, Dad said he had a surprise for me. I thought I was going to get a bike or a new C.D. player or something. I was just as happy to get what I did.

It was all the corn on the cob I could eat!

I would like to take a train ride every year.
Trains move faster than I thought they would.
She had brought her new gerbil along for the ride.

A Train Ride

When our family took its first train ride, my sister brought along a big box. She would not tell anyone what she had in it. In the middle of the trip, we heard a sound coming from the box. "Okay, Kate, now you have to open the box," said Mom. When she opened the box we were surprised.

She had brought her new gerbil along for the ride.

138 — Which Is Witch?

SPELLING

Homophones are words that sound the same but are spelled differently and have different meanings.

Directions: Use the homophones in the box to answer the riddles below.

main	peace	dear	to
mane	piece	deer	too

1. Which word has the word **pie** in it? **piece**

2. Which word rhymes with **ear** and is an animal? **deer**

3. Which word rhymes with **shoe** and means **also**? **too**

4. Which word has the same letters as the word **read** but in a different order? **dear**

5. Which word rhymes with **train** and is something on a pony? **mane**

6. Which word, if it began with a capital letter, might be the name of an important street? **main**

7. Which word sounds like a number but has only two letters? **to**

8. Which word rhymes with the last syllable in **police** and can mean quiet? **peace**

The Same but Different — 139

SPELLING

Directions: Write a word from the box to complete each sentence.

main	meat	dear	two
mane	meet	deer	too

1. The horse had a long, beautiful **mane**.
   The **main** idea of the paragraph was boats.

2. Let's **meet** at my house to do our homework.
   The lion was fed **meat** at mealtime.

3. We had **two** kittens.
   Jaden has a red bike. Tom does, **too**.

4. The **deer** ran in front of the car.
   I begin my letters with "**Dear** Mom."

140 — Let's Hear It for Homophones!

SPELLING

Directions: Circle the word in each sentence which is not spelled correctly. Then, write the word correctly.

1. Please (meat) me at the park. **meet**

2. I would like a (peace) of pie. **piece**

3. There were (too) cookies left. **two**

4. The horse's (main) needed to be brushed. **mane**

5. We saw a (dear) in the forest. **deer**

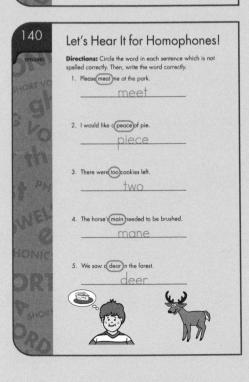

Busy Bees — 141

SPELLING

Directions: Cut out each honeybee at the bottom of the page and glue it on the flower with its homophone.

cut ✂-------------------------------------

Time to Rhyme! 143

Directions: Use homophones to create two-lined rhymes.

Example: I found it a **pain**
To comb the horse's **mane**!

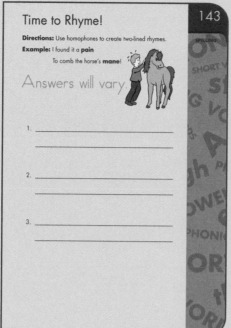

Answers will vary.

1. _____

_____

2. _____

_____

3. _____

_____

144 Clue Me In!

Short vowel patterns usually have a single vowel followed by a consonant sound.

Short a is the sound you hear in the word **can**.
Short e is the sound you hear in the word **men**.
Short i is the sound you hear in the word **pig**.
Short o is the sound you hear in the word **pot**.
Short u is the sound you hear in the word **truck**.

fast   track   spin   lunch   bread   block

Directions: Use the words in the box to answer the questions below.

Which word:

begins with the same sound as **blast** and ends with the same sound as **look**?   block

rhymes with **stack**?   track

begins with the same sound as **phone** and ends with the same sound as **lost**?   fast

has the same vowel sound as **hen**?   bread

rhymes with **crunch**?   lunch

begins with the same sound as **spot** and ends with the same sound as **can**?   spin

Picture This! 145

Directions: Use the words in the box to complete each sentence.

fast   wish   truck   bread   sun
best   stop   track   lunch   block

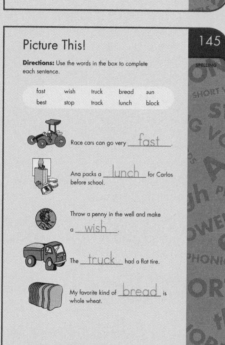

Race cars can go very ___fast___.

Ana packs a ___lunch___ for Carlos before school.

Throw a penny in the well and make a ___wish___.

The ___truck___ had a flat tire.

My favorite kind of ___bread___ is whole wheat.

146 Find It, Fix It

Directions: Circle the word in each sentence which is not spelled correctly. Then, write the word correctly.

1. Be sure to (stopp) at the red light.
___stop___

2. The train goes down the (trak).
___track___

3. Please put the (bred) in the toaster.
___bread___

4. I need another (blok) to finish.
___block___

5. The (beasst) player won a trophy.
___best___

6. Blow out the candles and make a (wiish).
___wish___

Say It Long 147

Long vowels are the letters **a, e, i, o** and **u** which say the letter name sound.

Long a is the sound you hear in **cane**.
Long e is the sound you hear in **green**.
Long i is the sound you hear in **pie**.
Long o is the sound you hear in **bowl**.
Long u is the sound you hear in **cube**.

lame   goal   pain   few   street
fright   nose   gray   bike   fuse

Directions: Use the words in the box to answer the questions below.

1. Add one letter to each of these words to make words from the box.

ray ___gray___   use ___fuse___
right ___fright___

2. Change one letter from each word to make a word from the box.

pail ___pain___   goat ___goal___
late ___lame___   bite ___bike___

3. Write the word from the box that . . .

has the long **e** sound.   street

rhymes with **you**.   few

is a homophone for **knows**.   nose

148 Getting A-Long with Vowels

Directions: Use the words in the box to complete each sentence.

goal   pain   few   bike
street   fright   nose   gray

1. Look both ways before crossing the ___street___.

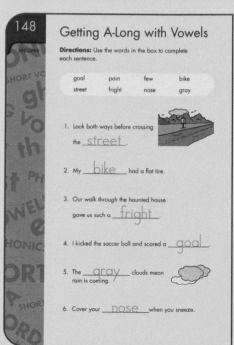

2. My ___bike___ had a flat tire.

3. Our walk through the haunted house gave us such a ___fright___.

4. I kicked the soccer ball and scored a ___goal___.

5. The ___gray___ clouds mean rain is coming.

6. Cover your ___nose___ when you sneeze.

Use the Clues! — 149

Directions: Use long vowel words from the box to answer the clues below. Write the letters of the words on the lines.

few	bike	dime	goal	fuse
lame	street	nose	fright	pain

1. f r i g h t (rhymes with **night**)
2. s t r e e t (could be Main or Maple)
3. f e w (synonym for **a couple**)
4. l a m e (rhymes with **tame**)
5. b i k e (can be ridden on a trail)
6. p a i n (homophone for **pane**)
7. d i m e (ten of these make a dollar)
8. g o a l (changing one letter of this word makes **goat**)
9. f u s e (has the word **use** in it)
10. n o s e (homophone for **knows**)

Now, read the letters in the boxes from top to bottom to find out what kind of a job you did!

tremendous

Pick a Word — 150

The **k** sound can be spelled with a **c**, **k** or **ck** after a short vowel sound.

Directions: Use the words from the box to complete the sentences. Use each word only once.

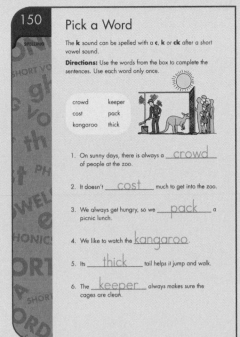

crowd	keeper
cost	pack
kangaroo	thick

1. On sunny days, there is always a crowd of people at the zoo.
2. It doesn't cost much to get into the zoo.
3. We always get hungry, so we pack a picnic lunch.
4. We like to watch the kangaroo.
5. Its thick tail helps it jump and walk.
6. The keeper always makes sure the cages are clean.

The Zoo's Kangaroos — 151

Directions: Use **c**, **k**, or **ck** words to complete this story. Some of the verbs are past tense and need to end with **ed**.

One day, Kevin and I packed 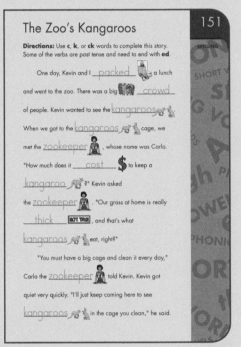 a lunch and went to the zoo. There was a big crowd of people. Kevin wanted to see the kangaroos. When we got to the kangaroos cage, we met the zookeeper, whose name was Carla.

"How much does it cost $ to keep a kangaroo?" Kevin asked the zookeeper. "Our grass at home is really thick, and that's what kangaroos eat, right?"

"You must have a big cage and clean it every day," Carla the zookeeper told Kevin. Kevin got quiet very quickly. "I'll just keep coming here to see kangaroos in the cage you clean," he said.

The Super Sounds of S — 152

The **s** sound can be spelled with an **s**, **ss**, **c** or **ce**.

Directions: Use the words from the box to complete the sentences below. Write each word only once.

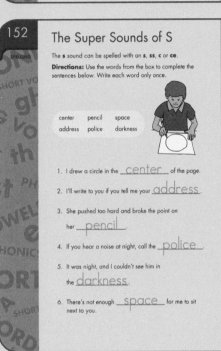

center	pencil	space
address	police	darkness

1. I drew a circle in the center of the page.
2. I'll write to you if you tell me your address.
3. She pushed too hard and broke the point on her pencil.
4. If you hear a noise at night, call the police.
5. It was night, and I couldn't see him in the darkness.
6. There's not enough space for me to sit next to you.

Sssspelling! — 153

Directions: Write the words from the box that answer the questions.

center pencil space address police darkness

1. Which words spell the **s** sound with **ss**?
   address   darkness
2. Which words spell **s** with a **c**?
   center   pencil
3. Which words spell **s** with **ce**?
   space   police
4. Write two other words you know that spell **s** with an **s**.
   Answers will vary
5. Put these letters in order to make words from the box.
   sdsdera   address
   sdserakn   darkness
   clipoe   police
   clipne   pencil
   capse   space
   retnce   center

Off to a Good Start — 154

Directions: Match each sentence with the word which completes it. Then, write the word on the line.

1. The farmer was unhappy because it didn't rain. → input
2. The scientist tried to discover secret formula. → unhappy
3. The child input his report into the computer. → disagree
4. We were unable to do the work without help. → replay
5. My brother and I disagree about which show to watch. → discover
6. The umpire called for a replay of the game. → inside
7. We had to stay inside when it got cold. → unable

That's the End! 155

A **suffix** is a word part added to the end of a word. Suffixes add to or change the meaning of the word.

Example: sad + ly = sadly

Below are some suffixes and their meanings.

ment	state of being, quality of, act of
ly	like or in a certain way
ness	state of being
ful	full of
less	without

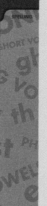

Directions: The words in the box have suffixes. Use the suffix meanings above to match each word with its meaning below. Write the words on the lines.

friendly cheerful safely sleeveless speechless
kindness amazement sickness peaceful excitement

1. in a safe way   s a f l e y
                              6

2. full of cheer   c h e e r f u l
                                    2

3. full of peace   p e a c e f u l
                              4

4. state of   a m a z e m e n t
   being amazed   5

5. state of   e x c i t e m e n t
   being excited   1

6. without speech s p e e c h l e s s
                                3

Use the numbered letters to find the missing word below. You are now on your way to becoming a

m a s t e r of suffixes!
5 6 3 1 4 2

Short and Sweet 156

A **contraction** is a short way to write two words together. Some letters are left out, but an apostrophe takes their place.

Directions: Write the words from the box that answer the questions.

hasn't   you've   aren't   we've   weren't

1. Write the correct contractions below.

Example:

I have	I've
was not	wasn't
we have	we've
you have	you've
are not	aren't
were not	weren't
has not	hasn't

2. Write two words from the box that are contractions using **have**.

you've   we've

3. Write three words from the box that are contractions using **not**.

hasn't   weren't

are'nt

Mad to Add 158

Directions: Add.

Example:

Add the ones.   Add the tens.

```
  26           26
 +21          +21
   7           47
```

```
  18      24      38      49      52
 +11     +35     +21     +50     +33
  29      59      59      99      85
```

```
  75      83      67      44      28
 +12     +16     +32     +25     +41
  87      99      99      69      69
```

68 + 20 = 88   54 + 25 = 79   71 + 17 = 88

The Lions scored 42 points. The Clippers scored 21 points. How many points were scored in all?

63

Sum It Up 159

Directions: Study the example. Add using regrouping.

Example:

```
  5,356
 +3,976
  9,332
```

Steps:
1. Add the ones.
2. Regroup the tens. Add the tens.
3. Regroup the hundreds. Add the hundreds.
4. Add the thousands.

```
  6,849         1,846         9,221
 +3,276        +8,384        +6,769
 10,125        10,230        15,990
```

```
  2,758         5,299         7,932
 +3,663        +8,764        +6,879
  6,421        14,063        14,811
```

A plane flew 1,838 miles on the first day. It flew 2,347 miles on the second day. How many miles did it fly in all?

4,185

Mental Math: Add On! 160

Directions: Try to do these addition problems in your head without using paper and pencil.

```
   7      6      8     10      2
  +4     +3     +1     +2     +9
  11      9      9     12     11
```

```
  10     40     80     60     50
 +20    +20   +100    +30    +70
  30     60    180     90    120
```

```
 350    300    400    450    680
+150   +500   +800    +10   +100
 500    800  1,200    460    780
```

```
         4,000    300   8,000
 1,000    400     200    500   9,800
+ 200   +  30   + 80   + 60  + 150
 1,200  4,430    580  8,560  9,950
```

What's the Difference? 161

Subtraction means "taking away" or subtracting one number from another to find the difference. For example, 10 - 3 = 7.

Directions: Subtract.

Example: Subtract the ones.   Subtract the tens.

```
   39            39
  -24           -24
    5            15
```

```
  48     95     87     55
 -35    -22    -16    -43
  13     73     71     12
```

```
  37     69     44     99
 -14    -57    -23    -78
  23     12     21     21
```

66 - 44 = 22   57 - 33 = 24

 The yellow car traveled 87 miles per hour. The orange car traveled 66 miles per hour. How much faster was the yellow car traveling?

21 mph

162 Ready to Regroup

Directions: Study the example. Add using regrouping.

Example:

$$\begin{array}{r} 634 \\ -455 \\ \hline 179 \end{array}$$

Steps:
1. Subtract ones. You cannot subtract five ones from 4 ones.
2. Regroup ones by regrouping 3 tens to 2 tens + 10 ones.
3. Subtract 5 ones from 14 ones.
4. Regroup tens by regrouping hundreds (5 hundreds + 10 tens).
5. Subtract 5 tens from 12 tens.
6. Subtract hundreds.

635	553	832	944	423
−169	−174	−563	−578	−268
466	379	269	366	155

941	733	266	387	594
−872	−498	−197	−198	−385
69	235	69	189	209

Bailey goes to school 185 days a year. Yoko goes to school 313 days a year. How many more days of school does Yoko attend each year?

128

163 Mental Math: Take It Away!

Directions: Try to do these subtraction problems in your head without using paper and pencil.

9	12	7	5	15
−3	− 6	−6	−1	− 5
6	6	1	4	10

40	90	100	20	60
−20	−80	− 50	−20	−10
20	10	50	0	50

450	500	250	690	320
−250	−300	− 20	−100	− 20
200	200	230	590	300

1,000	8,000	7,000	4,000	9,500
− 400	− 500	− 900	−2,000	−4,000
600	7,500	6,100	2,000	5,500

164 Round and Round We Go

If the ones number is 5 or greater, "round up" to the nearest 10. If the ones number is 4 or less, the tens number stays the same and the ones number becomes a zero.

Examples:

15 round up to 20

23 round down to 20

47 round up to 50

7	10	58	60
12	10	81	80
33	30	94	90
27	30	44	40
73	70	88	90
25	30	66	70
39	40	70	70

165 Round to the Right

If the tens number is 5 or greater, "round up" to the nearest hundred. If the tens number is 4 or less, the hundreds number remains the same.

REMEMBER. . . Look at the number directly to the right of the place to which you are rounding.

Examples:

230 round down to 200

150 round up to 200

470 round up to 500

732 round down to 700

456	500	120	100
340	300	923	900
867	900	550	600
686	700	231	200
770	800	492	500

166 Oh, My, Let's Multiply!

Multiplication is a short way to find the sum of adding the same number a certain amount of times. For example, we write $7 \times 4 = 28$ instead of $7 + 7 + 7 + 7 = 28$.

Directions: Study the example. Multiply.

Example:

There are two groups of seashells. There are 3 seashells in each group. How many seashells are there in all? $2 \times 3 = 6$

$4 + 4 = 8$ $3 + 3 + 3 = 9$
$2 \times 4 = 8$ $3 \times 3 = 9$

2	3	4	6	7
×3	×5	×3	×2	×3
6	15	12	12	21

5	6	4	7	8
×2	×3	×2	×2	×3
10	18	8	14	24

5	9	8	6	9
×5	×4	×5	×6	×3
25	36	40	36	27

167 Something's Fishy!

Factors are the numbers multiplied together in a multiplication problem. The answer is called the *product*. If you change the order of the factors, the product stays the same.

Example:

There are 4 groups of fish. There are 3 fish in each group. How many fish are there in all?

$4 \times 3 = 12$
factor × factor = product

Directions: Draw 3 groups of 4 fish.

$3 \times 4 = 12$

Compare your drawing and answer with the example. What did you notice?

Directions: Fill in the missing numbers. Multiply.

$5 \times 4 = 20$ $3 \times 6 = 18$ $4 \times 2 = 8$

$4 \times 5 = 20$ $6 \times 3 = 18$ $2 \times 4 = 8$

3	7	2	9	8	4
×7	×3	×9	×2	×4	×8
21	21	18	18	32	32

5	2	6	3	5	6
×2	×5	×3	×6	×6	×5
10	10	18	18	30	30

250

168 — Good Times!

MATH

Directions: Time yourself as you multiply. How quickly can you complete this page?

3 ×2 = 6	8 ×7 = 56	1 ×0 = 0	1 ×6 = 6	3 ×4 = 12
4 ×1 = 4	4 ×4 = 16	2 ×5 = 10	9 ×3 = 27	9 ×9 = 81
0 ×8 = 0	2 ×6 = 12	9 ×6 = 54	8 ×5 = 40	7 ×3 = 21
3 ×5 = 15	2 ×0 = 0	4 ×6 = 24	1 ×3 = 3	0 ×0 = 0

169 — Factor Facts

MATH

Directions: Complete the multiplication table. Use it to practice your multiplication facts.

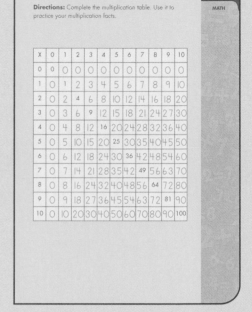

X	0	1	2	3	4	5	6	7	8	9	10
0	0	0	0	0	0	0	0	0	0	0	0
1	0	1	2	3	4	5	6	7	8	9	10
2	0	2	4	6	8	10	12	14	16	18	20
3	0	3	6	9	12	15	18	21	24	27	30
4	0	4	8	12	16	20	24	28	32	36	40
5	0	5	10	15	20	25	30	35	40	45	50
6	0	6	12	18	24	30	36	42	48	54	60
7	0	7	14	21	28	35	42	49	56	63	70
8	0	8	16	24	32	40	48	56	64	72	80
9	0	9	18	27	36	45	54	63	72	81	90
10	0	10	20	30	40	50	60	70	80	90	100

170 — Dare to Divide

MATH

Division is a way to find out how many times one number is contained in another number. For example, 28 ÷ 4 = 7 means that there are seven groups of four in 28.

Directions: Study the example. Divide.

Example:

There are 6 oars.
Each canoe needs 2 oars.
How many canoes can be used?
Circle groups of 2.
There are 3 groups of 2.

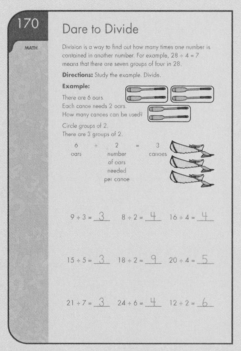

6	÷	2	=	3
oars		number of oars needed per canoe		canoes

9 ÷ 3 = 3   8 ÷ 2 = 4   16 ÷ 4 = 4

15 ÷ 5 = 3   18 ÷ 2 = 9   20 ÷ 4 = 5

21 ÷ 7 = 3   24 ÷ 6 = 4   12 ÷ 2 = 6

171 — Sail Away!

MATH

Directions: Divide. Draw a line from the boat to the sail with the correct answer.

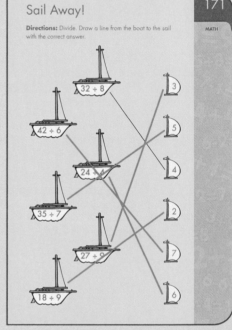

32 ÷ 8 → 4
42 ÷ 6 → 7
24 ÷ 4 → 6
35 ÷ 7 → 5
27 ÷ 9 → 3
18 ÷ 9 → 2

172 — Dive in to Division

MATH

Division is a way to find out how many times one number is contained in another number. The ÷ sign means "divided by." Another way to divide is to use ⟌. The dividend is the larger number that is divided by the smaller number, or divisor. The answer of a division problem is called the quotient.

Directions: Study the example. Divide.

Example:

20 ÷ 4 = 5
dividend divisor quotient

quotient
4⟌20
divisor dividend

35 ÷ 7 = 5   7⟌35   42 ÷ 6 = 7   6⟌42

2⟌12 = 6   3⟌18 = 6   4⟌36 = 9   5⟌50 = 10

6⟌24 = 4   7⟌21 = 3   8⟌32 = 4   9⟌27 = 3

36 ÷ 6 = 6   28 ÷ 4 = 7

15 ÷ 5 = 3   12 ÷ 2 = 6

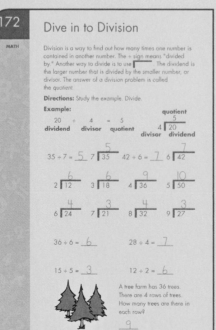

A tree farm has 36 trees. There are 4 rows of trees. How many trees are there in each row?

9

173 — What's Left?

MATH

Division is a way to find out how many times one number is contained in another number. For example, 28 ÷ 4 = 7 means that there are seven groups of four in 28. The dividend is the larger number that is divided by the smaller number, or divisor. The quotient is the answer in a division problem. The remainder is the amount left over. The remainder is always less than the divisor.

Directions: Study the example. Find each quotient and remainder.

Example:

There are 11 dog biscuits.
Put them in groups of 3.
There are 2 left over.

3
3⟌11

3 r2
3⟌11
−9
2 remainder

Remember: The remainder must be less than the **divisor!**

4 r1
3⟌13

4 r1
4⟌17

5 r2
6⟌32

5 r1
5⟌26

9 ÷ 4 = 2 r1   12 ÷ 5 = 2 r2

26 ÷ 4 = 6 r2   49 ÷ 9 = 5 r4

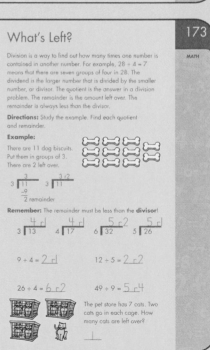

The pet store has 7 cats. Two cats go in each cage. How many cats are left over?

1

174

Rules to Remember

A number is divisible...

by 2 if the last digit is 0 or even (2, 4, 6, 8).
by 3 if the sum of all digits is divisible by 3.
by 4 if the last two digits are divisible by 4.
by 5 if the last digit is a 0 or 5.
by 10 if the last digit is 0.

Example: 250 is divisible by 2, 5, 10

Directions: Tell what numbers each of these numbers is divisible by.

3,732 2 3 4   439 —

50 2 5 10   444 2 3 4

7,960 2 4 5 10   8,212 2 4

104,924 2 4   2,345 5

175

Factor Trees

Factors are the smaller numbers multiplied together to make a larger number. Factor trees are one way to find all the factors of a number.

Example:

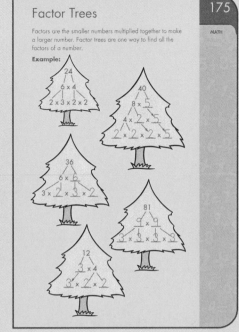

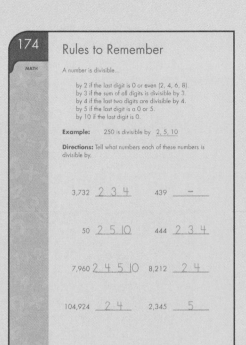

176

Following Orders

When you solve a problem that involves more than one operation, this is the order to follow:

( ) Parentheses first
x   Multiplication
÷   Division
+   Addition
−   Subtraction

Example:

2 + (3 x 5) - 2 = 15
2 + 15 - 2 = 15
17 - 2 = 15

Directions: Solve the problems using the correct order of operations.

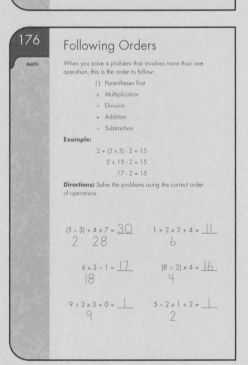

(5 − 3) + 4 x 7 = 30
  2   28

1 + 2 x 3 + 4 = 11
        6

6 x 3 − 1 = 17
  18

(8 ÷ 2) x 4 = 16
      4

9 ÷ 3 x 3 + 0 = 1
    9

5 − 2 x 1 + 2 = 1
        2

177

Let's Operate!

Directions: Use +, −, x and ÷ to complete the problems so the number sentence is true.

Example: 4 **+** 2 **−** 1 = 5

(8 **÷** 2) **+** 4 = 8

(1 **+** 2) **÷** 3 = 1

9 **+** 3 **−** 9 = 3

REMEMBER...
USE THE ORDER OF OPERATIONS

(7 **−** 5) **X** 1 = 2

8 **X** 5 **÷** 4 = 10

5 **−** 4 **÷** 1 = 1

178

Perfect Percentages

A percentage is the amount of a number out of 100. This is the percent sign: %

Directions: Fill in the blanks.

Example: 70% = $\frac{70}{100}$ **40**% = $\frac{40}{100}$

30% = $\frac{30}{100}$ 10% = $\frac{10}{100}$

90% = $\frac{90}{100}$ 40% = $\frac{40}{100}$

70% = $\frac{70}{100}$ 80% = $\frac{80}{100}$

20% = $\frac{20}{100}$ **60**% = $\frac{60}{100}$

30% = $\frac{30}{100}$ **10**% = $\frac{10}{100}$

50% = $\frac{50}{100}$ **90**% = $\frac{90}{100}$

179

Pick the Parts

A fraction is a number that names part of a whole, such as $\frac{1}{2}$ or $\frac{1}{4}$.

Directions: Write the fraction that tells what part of each figure is colored. The first one is done for you.

Example:

2 parts shaded
5 parts in the whole figure

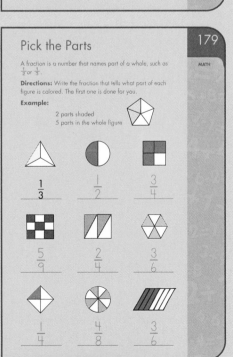

$\frac{1}{3}$ $\frac{1}{2}$ $\frac{3}{4}$

$\frac{5}{9}$ $\frac{2}{4}$ $\frac{3}{6}$

$\frac{1}{4}$ $\frac{4}{8}$ $\frac{3}{6}$

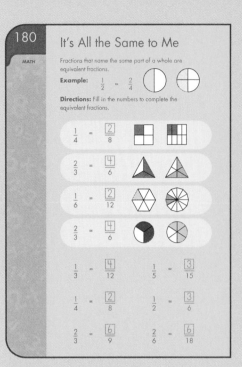

180 · It's All the Same to Me

Fractions that name the same part of a whole are equivalent fractions.

Example: $\frac{1}{2} = \frac{2}{4}$

Directions: Fill in the numbers to complete the equivalent fractions.

$\frac{1}{4} = \frac{2}{8}$

$\frac{2}{3} = \frac{4}{6}$

$\frac{1}{6} = \frac{2}{12}$

$\frac{2}{3} = \frac{4}{6}$

$\frac{1}{3} = \frac{4}{12}$ $\frac{1}{5} = \frac{3}{15}$

$\frac{1}{4} = \frac{2}{8}$ $\frac{1}{2} = \frac{3}{6}$

$\frac{2}{3} = \frac{6}{9}$ $\frac{2}{6} = \frac{6}{18}$

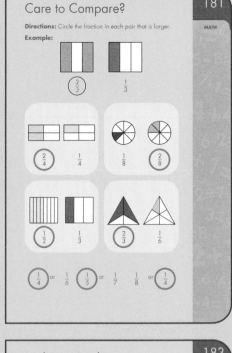

181 · Care to Compare?

Directions: Circle the fraction in each pair that is larger.

Example:

$\frac{2}{3}$ $\frac{1}{3}$

$\frac{2}{4}$ $\frac{1}{4}$ $\frac{1}{8}$ $\frac{2}{8}$

$\frac{1}{2}$ $\frac{1}{3}$ $\frac{2}{3}$ $\frac{1}{6}$

$\frac{1}{4}$ or $\frac{1}{6}$ $\frac{1}{5}$ or $\frac{1}{7}$ $\frac{1}{8}$ or $\frac{1}{4}$

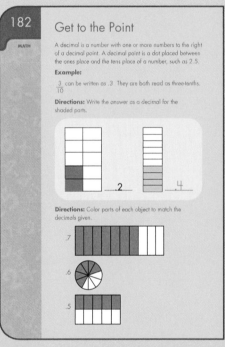

182 · Get to the Point

A decimal is a number with one or more numbers to the right of a decimal point. A decimal point is a dot placed between the ones place and the tens place of a number, such as 2.5.

Example:

$\frac{3}{10}$ can be written as .3 They are both read as three-tenths.

Directions: Write the answer as a decimal for the shaded parts.

.2   .4

Directions: Color parts of each object to match the decimals given.

.7

.6

.5

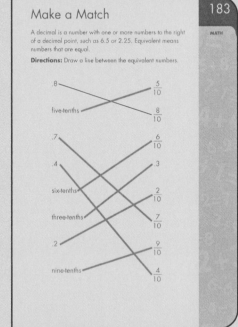

183 · Make a Match

A decimal is a number with one or more numbers to the right of a decimal point, such as 6.5 or 2.25. Equivalent means numbers that are equal.

Directions: Draw a line between the equivalent numbers.

.8 — $\frac{5}{10}$

five-tenths — $\frac{8}{10}$

.7 — $\frac{6}{10}$

.4 — 3

six-tenths — $\frac{2}{10}$

three-tenths — $\frac{7}{10}$

.2 — $\frac{9}{10}$

nine-tenths — $\frac{4}{10}$

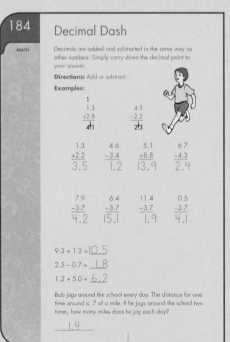

184 · Decimal Dash

Decimals are added and subtracted in the same way as other numbers. Simply carry down the decimal point to your answer.

Directions: Add or subtract.

Examples:

$\begin{array}{r} 1 \\ 1.3 \\ +2.8 \\ \hline 4.1 \end{array}$ $\begin{array}{r} 4.5 \\ -2.2 \\ \hline 2.3 \end{array}$

$\begin{array}{r} 1.3 \\ +2.2 \\ \hline 3.5 \end{array}$ $\begin{array}{r} 4.6 \\ -3.4 \\ \hline 1.2 \end{array}$ $\begin{array}{r} 5.1 \\ +8.8 \\ \hline 13.9 \end{array}$ $\begin{array}{r} 6.7 \\ -4.3 \\ \hline 2.4 \end{array}$

$\begin{array}{r} 7.9 \\ -3.7 \\ \hline 4.2 \end{array}$ $\begin{array}{r} 6.4 \\ -3.7 \\ \hline 15.1 \end{array}$ $\begin{array}{r} 11.4 \\ -3.7 \\ \hline 1.9 \end{array}$ $\begin{array}{r} 0.5 \\ -3.7 \\ \hline 4.1 \end{array}$

$9.3 + 1.2 = 10.5$

$2.5 - 0.7 = 1.8$

$1.2 + 5.0 = 6.2$

Bob jogs around the school every day. The distance for one time around is .7 of a mile. If he jogs around the school two times, how many miles does he jog each day?

1.4

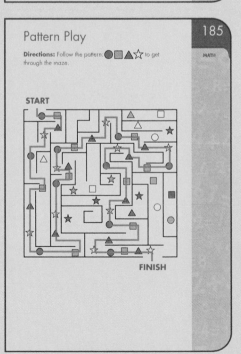

185 · Pattern Play

Directions: Follow the pattern ● ■ ▲ ☆ to get through the maze.

START

FINISH

186 — Crack the Color Code!

Geometry is the branch of mathematics that has to do with points, lines and shapes.

cube rectangular prism cone cylinder sphere

Directions: Use the code to color the picture.

Color:
cubes = **blue**
rectangular prisms = **red**
cones = green
cylinders = yellow
spheres = orange

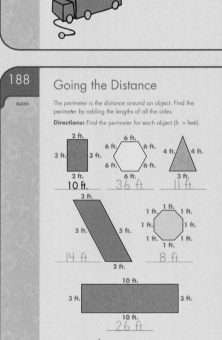

187 — Get in Line!

Geometry is the branch of mathematics that has to do with points, lines and shapes.

A **line** goes on and on in both directions. It has no end points.

⎯⎯ Line CD

A **segment** is part of a line. It has two end points.

⎯⎯ Segment AB

A **ray** has a line segment with only one end point. It goes on and on in the other direction.

⎯⎯ Ray EF

An **angle** has two rays with the same end point.

Angle BAC

Directions: Write the name for each figure.

line ray
segment line
angle line

188 — Going the Distance

The perimeter is the distance around an object. Find the perimeter by adding the lengths of all the sides.

Directions: Find the perimeter for each object (ft. = feet).

10 ft. 36 ft 11 ft

14 ft 8 ft

26 ft

17 ft 10 ft

189 — All Around Town

A **map scale** shows how far one place is from another. This map scale shows that 1 inch on this page equals 1 mile at the real location.

Directions: Use a ruler and the map scale to find out how far it is from Ann's house to other places. Round to the nearest mile.

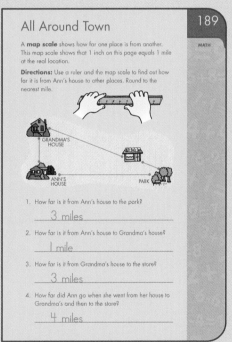

1. How far is it from Ann's house to the park? 3 miles
2. How far is it from Ann's house to Grandma's house? 1 mile
3. How far is it from Grandma's house to the store? 3 miles
4. How far did Ann go when she went from her house to Grandma's and then to the store? 4 miles

190 — Blast Off!

Directions: Answer the questions about the graph.

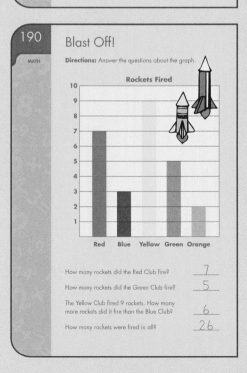

How many rockets did the Red Club fire? 7
How many rockets did the Green Club fire? 5
The Yellow Club fired 9 rockets. How many more rockets did it fire than the Blue Club? 6
How many rockets were fired in all? 26

191 — Weigh In

Ounces and pounds are measurements of weight in the standard measurement system. The ounce is used to measure the weight of very light objects. The pound is used to measure the weight of heavier objects. 16 ounces = 1 pound.

Example: 8 ounces 15 pounds

Directions: Decide if you would use ounces or pounds to measure the weight of each object. Circle your answer.

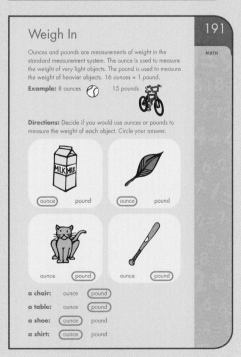

ounce / pound ounce / pound
ounce / pound ounce / pound

a chair: ounce / **pound**
a table: ounce / **pound**
a shoe: **ounce** / pound
a shirt: **ounce** / pound

192 — Inching Along

MATH

An inch is a unit of length in the standard measurement system.

Directions: Use a ruler to measure each object to the nearest $\frac{1}{4}$ inch. Write **in.** to stand for inch.

Example:

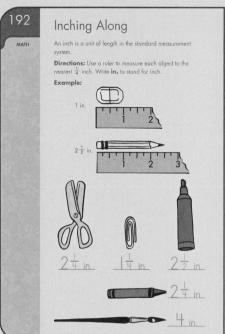

1 in.

$2\frac{1}{2}$ in.

$2\frac{1}{4}$ in. $1\frac{1}{4}$ in. $2\frac{1}{2}$ in.

$2\frac{1}{4}$ in.

4 in.

193 — Centimeter Sense

A centimeter is a unit of length in the metric system. There are 2.54 centimeters in an inch.

Directions: Use a centimeter ruler to measure each object to the nearest half a centimeter. Write **cm** to stand for centimeter.

Example:

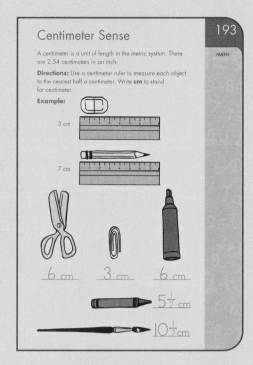

3 cm

7 cm

6 cm   3 cm   6 cm

$5\frac{1}{2}$ cm

$10\frac{1}{2}$ cm

194 — Measuring Up: Foot, Yard, Mile

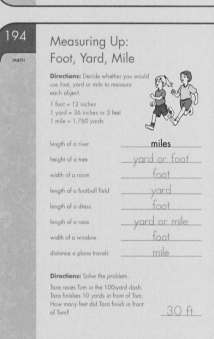

Directions: Decide whether you would use foot, yard or mile to measure each object.

1 foot = 12 inches
1 yard = 36 inches or 3 feet
1 mile = 1,760 yards

length of a river	miles
height of a tree	yard or foot
width of a room	foot
length of a football field	yard
length of a dress	foot
length of a race	yard or mile
width of a window	foot
distance a plane travels	mile

Directions: Solve the problem.

Tara races Tom in the 100-yard dash. Tara finishes 10 yards in front of Tom. How many feet did Tara finish in front of Tom?

30 ft

195 — Measuring Up: Meter and Kilometer

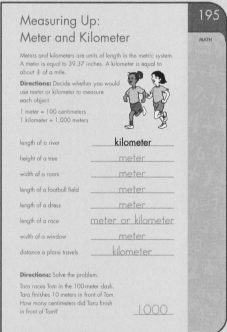

Meters and kilometers are units of length in the metric system. A meter is equal to 39.37 inches. A kilometer is equal to about $\frac{5}{8}$ of a mile.

Directions: Decide whether you would use meter or kilometer to measure each object.

1 meter = 100 centimeters
1 kilometer = 1,000 meters

length of a river	kilometer
height of a tree	meter
width of a room	meter
length of a football field	meter
length of a dress	meter
length of a race	meter or kilometer
width of a window	meter
distance a plane travels	kilometer

Directions: Solve the problem.

Tara races Tom in the 100-meter dash. Tara finishes 10 meters in front of Tom. How many centimeters did Tara finish in front of Tom?

1000

196 — Counting Back in Time

Another way to write numbers is to use Roman numerals.

I	1	VII	7
II	2	VIII	8
III	3	IX	9
IV	4	X	10
V	5	XI	11
VI	6	XII	12

Directions: Fill in the Roman numerals on the watch.

What time is it on the watch?

3:00 o'clock

197 — Do You Have the Time?

Directions: Write the time shown on each clock.

Example:

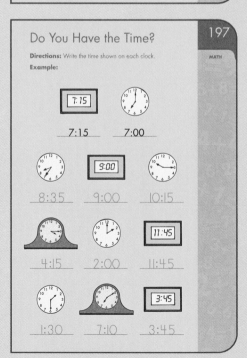

7:15   7:00

8:35   9:00   10:15

4:15   2:00   11:45

1:30   7:10   3:45

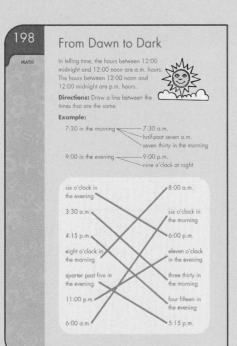

198 From Dawn to Dark

MATH

In telling time, the hours between 12:00 midnight and 12:00 noon are a.m. hours. The hours between 12:00 noon and 12:00 midnight are p.m. hours.

Directions: Draw a line between the times that are the same.

Example:

7:30 in the morning — 7:30 a.m.
— half-past seven a.m.
— seven thirty in the morning

9:00 in the evening — 9:00 p.m.
— nine o'clock at night

six o'clock in the evening — 8:00 a.m.
3:30 a.m. — six o'clock in the morning
4:15 p.m. — 6:00 p.m.
eight o'clock in the morning — eleven o'clock in the evening
quarter past five in the evening — three thirty in the morning
11:00 p.m. — four fifteen in the evening
6:00 a.m. — 5:15 p.m.

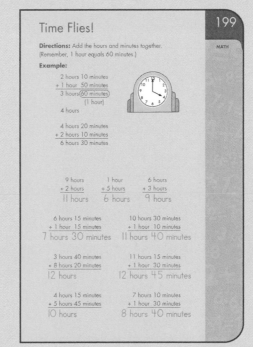

199 Time Flies!

MATH

Directions: Add the hours and minutes together. (Remember, 1 hour equals 60 minutes.)

Example:

```
  2 hours 10 minutes
+ 1 hour  50 minutes
  3 hours 60 minutes
          (1 hour)
  4 hours
```

```
  4 hours 20 minutes
+ 2 hours 10 minutes
  6 hours 30 minutes
```

```
  9 hours       1 hour       6 hours
+ 2 hours     + 5 hours    + 3 hours
 11 hours      6 hours      9 hours
```

```
  6 hours 15 minutes      10 hours 30 minutes
+ 1 hour  15 minutes    +  1 hour  10 minutes
  7 hours 30 minutes      11 hours 40 minutes
```

```
  3 hours 40 minutes      11 hours 15 minutes
+ 8 hours 20 minutes    +  1 hour  30 minutes
 12 hours                12 hours 45 minutes
```

```
  4 hours 15 minutes       7 hours 10 minutes
+ 5 hours 45 minutes    +  1 hour  30 minutes
 10 hours                 8 hours 40 minutes
```

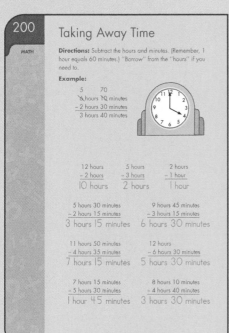

200 Taking Away Time

MATH

Directions: Subtract the hours and minutes. (Remember, 1 hour equals 60 minutes.) "Borrow" from the "hours" if you need to.

Example:

```
  5      70
  6 hours 10 minutes
- 2 hours 30 minutes
  3 hours 40 minutes
```

```
 12 hours      5 hours      2 hours
- 2 hours    - 3 hours    - 1 hour
 10 hours      2 hours      1 hour
```

```
  5 hours 30 minutes       9 hours 45 minutes
- 2 hours 15 minutes     - 3 hours 15 minutes
  3 hours 15 minutes       6 hours 30 minutes
```

```
 11 hours 50 minutes      12 hours
-  4 hours 35 minutes    - 6 hours 30 minutes
  7 hours 15 minutes      5 hours 30 minutes
```

```
  7 hours 15 minutes       8 hours 10 minutes
- 5 hours 30 minutes     - 4 hours 40 minutes
  1 hour 45 minutes        3 hours 30 minutes
```

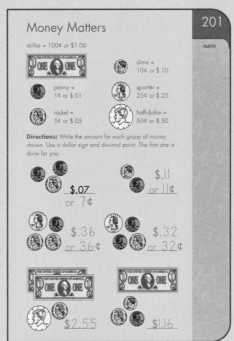

201 Money Matters

MATH

dollar = 100¢ or $1.00

penny = 1¢ or $.01
nickel = 5¢ or $.05
dime = 10¢ or $.10
quarter = 25¢ or $.25
half-dollar = 50¢ or $.50

Directions: Write the amount for each group of money shown. Use a dollar sign and decimal point. The first one is done for you.

$.07 or 7¢

$.11 or 11¢

$.36 or 36¢

$.32 or 32¢

$2.55

$1.16

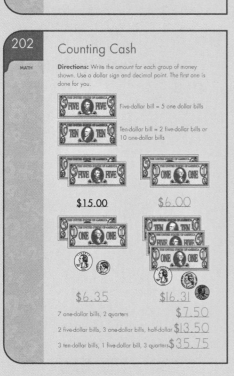

202 Counting Cash

MATH

Directions: Write the amount for each group of money shown. Use a dollar sign and decimal. The first one is done for you.

Five-dollar bill = 5 one dollar bills

Ten-dollar bill = 2 five-dollar bills or 10 one-dollar bills

$15.00

$6.00

$6.35

$16.31

7 one-dollar bills, 2 quarters $7.50

2 five-dollar bills, 3 one-dollar bills, half-dollar $13.50

3 ten-dollar bills, 1 five-dollar bill, 3 quarters $35.75

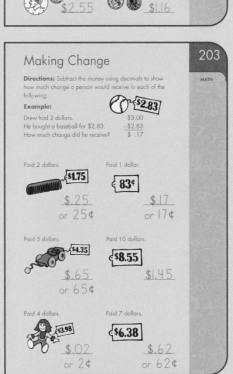

203 Making Change

MATH

Directions: Subtract the money using decimals to show how much change a person would receive in each of the following.

Example:

$2.83

Drew had 3 dollars.
He bought a baseball for $2.83.
How much change did he receive?

```
 $3.00
-$2.83
 $ .17
```

Paid 2 dollars. $1.75
$.25 or 25¢

Paid 1 dollar. 83¢
$.17 or 17¢

Paid 5 dollars. $4.35
$.65 or 65¢

Paid 10 dollars. $8.55
$1.45

Paid 4 dollars. $3.98
$.02 or 2¢

Paid 7 dollars. $6.38
$.62 or 62¢

204 Fun Fair!

Directions: Read and solve each problem. The first one is done for you.

The clown started the day with 200 balloons. He gave away 128 of them. Some broke. At the end of the day he had 18 balloons left. How many of the balloons broke?   **54**

On Monday, there were 925 tickets sold to adults and 1,412 tickets sold to children. How many more children attended the fair than adults?   487

At one game booth, prizes were given out for scoring 500 points in three attempts. Sanj scored 178 points on her first attempt, 149 points on her second attempt and 233 points on her third attempt. Did Sanj win a prize?   yes

The prize-winning steer weighed 2,348 pounds. The runner-up steer weighed 2,179 pounds. How much more did the prize steer weigh?   169 pounds

205 Eat Your Veggies!

Directions: Read and solve each problem.

Jeff and Riley are planting a garden. They plant 3 rows of green beans with 8 plants in each row. How many green bean plants are there in the garden?   24

There are 45 tomato plants in the garden. There are 5 rows of them. How many tomato plants are in each row?   9

The children have 12 plants each of lettuce, broccoli and spinach. How many plants are there in all?   36

Jeff planted 3 times as many cucumber plants as Riley. He planted 15 of them. How many did Riley plant?   5

Riley planted 12 pepper plants. He planted twice as many green pepper plants as red pepper plants. How many green pepper plants are there?   8

206 Farm Living

A fraction is a number that names part of a whole, such as ½ or ⅓.

Directions: Read and solve each problem.

There are 20 large animals on the Browns' farm. Two-fifths are horses, two-fifths are cows and the rest are pigs. Are there more pigs or cows on the farm?   cows

Farmer Brown had 40 eggs to sell. He sold half of them in the morning. In the afternoon, he sold half of what was left. How many eggs did Farmer Brown have at the end of the day?   10

There is a fence running around seven-tenths of the farm. How much of the farm does not have a fence around it? Write the amount as a decimal.   .3

The Browns have 10 chickens. Two are roosters and the rest are hens. Write a decimal for the number that are roosters and for the number that are hens.   .2 roosters   .8 hens

207 A Race to the Finish

Directions: Read and solve each problem.

This year, hundreds of people ran in the Capital City Marathon. The race is 4.2 kilometers long. When the first person crossed the finish line, the last person was at the 3.7 kilometer point. How far ahead was the winner?   .5

Hasaan crossed the finish line 10 meters ahead of Lucy. Lucy was 5 meters ahead of Sam. How far ahead of Sam was Hasaan?   15

Tony ran 320 yards from school to his home. Then, he ran 290 yards to Jay's house. Together Tony and Jay ran 545 yards to the store. How many yards in all did Tony run?   1155

The teacher measured the heights of three children in her class. Gabriella was 51 inches tall, Jimmy was 48 inches tall and Deepak was 52½ inches tall. How much taller is Deepak than Gabriella? $1\frac{1}{2}$ in.

×	0	1	2	3	4	5	6	7	8	9	10
4	0	4	8	12	16	20	24	28	32	36	40
5	0	5	10	15	20	25	30	35	40	45	50
6	0	6	12	18	24	30	36	42	48	54	60
7	0	7	14	21	28	35	42	49	56	63	70
8	0	8	16	24	32	40	48	56	64	72	80
9	0	9	18	27	36	45	54	63	72	81	90
10	0	10	20	30	40	50	60	70	80	90	100

Multiplication Table

X	0	1	2	3	4	5	6	7	8	9	10
0	0	0	0	0	0	0	0	0	0	0	0
1	0	1	2	3	4	5	6	7	8	9	10
2	0	2	4	6	8	10	12	14	16	18	20
3	0	3	6	9	12	15	18	21	24	27	30